CONQUER ANXIETY

HOW TO OVERCOME ANXIETY AND OPTIMIZE YOUR PERFORMANCE

Praise for *Conquer Anxiety*

"This book offers practical, easy-to-understand strategies for managing performance anxiety and beyond. The Five Stages of Peak Performance are based on research-tested approaches and have yielded effective results with countless performers over decades of implementation. The activities in this workbook can be practiced in small bits or large chunks according to individual need and are flexible enough to be visited (and revisited) multiple times to reinforce positive, self-supporting habits."

KARIN S. HENDRICKS, PhD – Associate Professor and Chair of Music Education, Boston University; Author of *Performance Anxiety Strategies and Compassionate Music Teaching*

"This terrific book will provide anyone with the knowledge and skill to handle and regulate anxiety. Even more important is that it inspires personal growth and provides a model for living one's best - not just for surviving but for thriving."

JUDITH SCHWEIGER LEVY, PhD – Clinical Psychologist

"This book is a must read for any performer who is serious about their success. It will help anyone who has ever felt anxiety to move forward, gain a greater sense of peace, and be able to deliver an outstanding performance."

JENNY OAKS BAKER – America's Violinist, Grammy Nominated, Billboard No. 1 Recording Artist, and Performer

"Finally, anxiety has met its match! Reading this book has enlightened my awareness of the destructive effects of anxiety itself and instilled the confidence that it doesn't have to accompany our daily performance anymore. The authors form a dynamic team of expertise who provide the proper mindset and skill set required to conquer anxiety. This book and its applied processes will bless anyone to live a life of peace and balance."

THOMAS BLACKWELL – Author, International Speaker, and Peak Performance Coach

"Since hearing about this research on performance anxiety, I have continued to use these materials in my own teaching. Now having all of these "helps" in one place is the best of all possible worlds! *Conquer Anxiety* offers an empathetic and personable approach to helping students, teachers, performing artists, and those in the business world reach their full potential and peak performance. Hallelujah for this book to help us ALL Conquer Anxiety."

LINDA POETSCHKE – Cofounder and Program Director of the Taos Opera Institute and Professor Emeritus of Music University of Texas at San Antonio

"*Conquer Anxiety* unfolds like a treasure map, a step by step guide to uncover the potential buried within you. Don't let doubt and insecurity pirate your passion. Instead, use this program to navigate negativity and chart a positive course to your future self: A gifted performer who enrichens every audience!"

MARK BAXTER – World-Renowned Vocal Coach, voicelesson.com

"Fear and anxiety are perhaps the biggest barriers we face to almost everything we want. Getting past anxiety stands as an enormous and overwhelming task to most. With years of experience in professional psychology and performance coaching, the authors of *Conquer Anxiety* give us an owner's manual for how to operate the equipment of our own brain. More than conquering anxiety, this manual helps us to reframe it in a way that activates our brain, and our potential. This book could very well be the key you are looking for to unlock your power to succeed."

PAUL H. JENKINS, PhD – Psychologist and Author of *Pathological Positivity*

"*Conquer Anxiety* is full of powerful principles and useful exercises that can help anyone take control of their thinking and perform at their very best."

DAVE CRENSHAW – Author of *The Result: The Practical, Proven Formula for Getting What You Want*

"Anxiety is real. Today, over half of the illnesses in America are stress related. Anyone who feels stressed or overwhelmed NEEDS TO READ THIS BOOK, as it provides not only a blueprint on how to come to terms with anxiety, but also how to CONQUER anxiety."

DANNY BRASSELL, PhD – Internationally Acclaimed Speaker, Best-Selling Author of *Sixteen Books* and Co-Creator of ReadBETTERin67Steps.com

"If I had read and studied this amazing *Conquer Anxiety* when I was a young adult, I would have been a better athlete, a more focused student and a much more accomplished human being. The authors not only teach you the Five Stages of Peak Performance, but they have created a strategic 'playbook' and inspirational reference guide to help us all face our fears, rise to every occasion and operate at maximum capacity."

DAN CLARK – Hall of Fame Speaker, Author of *The Art of Significance*

"If you want to overcome obstacles and live your best life, then read and absorb the strategies in this brilliant book! This book should be required reading as it has the power to change your life!"

JAMES MALINCHAK – Featured on ABCs Hit TV Show, "Secret Millionaire," Two-Time National College Speaker of the Year, and Author of *Millionaire Success Secrets*

CONQUER ANXIETY

HOW TO OVERCOME ANXIETY AND OPTIMIZE YOUR PERFORMANCE

JON SKIDMORE PSY.D.   ROB SHALLENBERGER

STEVEN SHALLENBERGER

First Edition

ISBN 978-0-9888459-7-8

For information regarding special discounts for bulk purchases, please contact Becoming Your Best Global Leadership at (888) 690-8764 or Support@ BecomingYourBest.com.

Dedication

To those courageous souls seeking the freedom to sing their songs, share their messages, and give their gifts.

— DR. JON SKIDMORE

To all those people in the world who desire to become their best and conquer one more thing that stands in the way: anxiety. You can do it and make every day and each performance among your best!

—STEVEN SHALLENBERGER

This book is dedicated to those willing to get in the arena—which can be a tough place to be—and make improvements to their life.

— ROB SHALLENBERGER

Contents

Preface

The breakthrough research you'll find in *Conquer Anxiety* gives you a clear pathway on how to achieve hope, confidence, peace, and control in every aspect of your life. If you or someone you know has experienced anxiety, you know firsthand how debilitating it can be. We've developed the Five Stages of Peak Performance to give people a simple way to understand their anxiety and move forward.

Oliver Wendell Holmes once stated, "I wouldn't give a fig for the simplicity on this side of complexity, but I would give my right arm for the simplicity on the far side of complexity."

In this book, you get seventy-five rich, combined years of research and experience from the authors, who break down complex ideas and present solutions in a simple, easy-to-understand format. These life-changing ideas will liberate you to perform at your highest level throughout life. The sooner you learn about and start using the tools found in the Five Stages, the sooner you will experience their powerful benefits.

I especially want to thank Dr. Jon Skidmore and Rob Shallenberger for their extraordinary talent and writing skills, which have translated into making this subject manageable and approachable. I sat in on review meetings for well over a year as the book came together. This magnificent team has taken intense research, scientific data, one-on-one interviews, and years of classroom experience and put it all into a simple, powerful format anyone can use.

When I was twelve years old, I gave my first talk to a church congregation of over two hundred. I meticulously wrote that talk on ten three-by-five cards, then practiced reading it so I wouldn't stumble over my words. The day came, and as I nervously walked up to the pulpit, it felt like my heart was going to jump right out of my chest it was pounding so hard. I started reading the cards, and everything seemed to be going well—until I finished with card six. To my dismay, card seven was missing. In front of the entire congregation, I started searching for the missing card, shuffling through my pile of cards and then going through each of my pockets. It was awkward for everyone in the congregation and even more awkward for me, and, in total embarrassment, I sat down without finishing my talk. I was in tears. Fortunately, people kindly patted me on the back and thanked me for a lovely message.

And what appeared to be a disaster actually became a great learning opportunity. If I'd known about the Five Stages as a young man, it would have transformed the way I'd approached this whole situation and saved me a lot of emotional turmoil. This pivotal experience has helped me relate to so many who experience anxiety at varying degrees.

Just as they have for me, the Five Stages will teach you how to take your past experiences, learn from them, build on them, and consistently get better at what you do. They will help you deal with your feelings of anxiety and know what you can do to optimize any performance.

Conquer Anxiety is a book every performer (e.g., musician, actor, athlete, etc.), coach, teacher, and parent should own and share with their children, grandchildren, fellow team members, and students.

How to Get the Most from This Book

Below are three ideas to help you to get the most from *Conquer Anxiety*.

First, don't just read the book. Complete the activities and write down your thoughts. There will be a lot of places where we ask you to write and share your experiences and ideas. Don't skip these. It's like anything else: what you put into it is what you get out of it.

These activities and questions can have a huge impact on your life if you take the time to complete and answer them.

Second, share the powerful ideas and techniques you learn here with loved ones, friends, and professional associates. Whenever you teach something, you are the one who learns the most. The idea is that the student becomes the teacher and helps the people who matter most in their life.

Third, discuss and apply the Five Stages with others. While it's true that you will experience huge gains by practicing the ideas in this book, you'll progress even more if you share the journey with a trusted mentor, coach, or friend. Those you have close relationships with can often help you see things you can't see with your current mindset and perspective.

As Teddy Roosevelt once astutely observed, "It is not the critic who counts; not the man who points out how the strong man stumbles, or where the doer of deeds could have done them better. The credit belongs to the person who is actually in the arena, whose face is marred by dust and sweat and blood; . . . who at the worst, if he fails, at least fails while daring greatly, so that his place shall never be with those cold and timid souls who neither know victory nor defeat."

Congratulations for stepping into the arena and being willing to improve your life. The arena of life isn't an easy place to be. A lot of people prefer to avoid it. But not you! You've taken the most important step because you want to make changes. You're willing to look at things in a new way and try new ideas. You're willing to share your talents and gifts to make the world a better place.

We're confident *Conquer Anxiety* and the Five Stages will have a huge impact on your life and give you a whole new set of tools as you strive to become your best!

—STEVEN SHALLENBERGER, AUTHOR of the
National Best-Selling Book: *Becoming Your Best:
The 12 Principles of Highly Successful Leaders*

Acknowledgments

S ir Isaac Newton once said, "If I have seen further than others, it is by standing upon the shoulders of giants."

We are grateful for the giants in our lives who contributed to help bring about Conquer Anxiety. Because there are so many people who have helped bring this book to fruition, it would be impossible to name them all. However, we would like to highlight a few of the key people who were instrumental in helping make it a reality:

First, I would like to thank my father, C. Jay Skidmore, PhD, who was a psychologist, and my mother, Anna Jean Skidmore, MA, who was a musician. Their legacy lives on in everything I do. A special thanks to my amazing wife, Kathy, and my children, TJ, Amber, Kali and Jonathan, for their constant support and faith in my vision. I express a grateful and a sincere thanks to Jamie Thorup, who saw the possibility of what I have to share and connected me with Steve and Rob Shallenberger. I am grateful for their commitment and passion to Becoming Your Best. Without the expertise, persistence, and patience of Steve and Rob, this book would still be waiting "safely" in the realm of good ideas. And thanks to Scott and Vicki Thorpe, whose enduring friendship, example, and coaching have been vital to the development and completion of this book. To Paul Broomhead, PhD, for his partnership in our research projects. To Newell Dayley, former dean of the BYU school of music, who was willing to let me bring Music 259, the Psychology of Music Performance, to countless talented young musicians. To the innumerable courageous Brigham Young University students who thought they were taking a class on performance psychology but unknowingly walked into a laboratory for the development of this book. And to the many others who each in their unique way have powerfully influenced me and this book: Judith Levey; Dave Crenshaw; Mark Baxter; Linda Poetschke; Larry Skidmore; Norma Jean Remington, PhD; Paul Jenkins, PhD; Doug Hoyt; Bill Wilson; Karin Hendricks; and Russell Jenkins: your contribution has been invaluable to this book.

And thank you to the thousands of workshop participants, both young and old, who have wanted to share with the world their gifts and who have found the freedom to do so.

—JON

There are so many influencers in my life who were instrumental in helping with this book. As always, I need to acknowledge my wife, Tonya, and our amazing children, Robbie, Bella, Lana, and Clara. In addition, my parents and siblings continue to play a huge role in my life. Among so many amazing people, there were several who provided great feedback and ideas. They include Gary Marlowe, Lara Baker, Megan Riley, Brandon Erickson, Dr. David Glen Hatch, and Katie McKnight.

—ROB

To the remarkable associates and friends at Becoming Your Best: Jamie Thorup, Thomas Blackwell, Murphy Smith, Carli Sorenson, Danielle Moran, Anne S. Peterson, Lara Shallenberger, Tommy Shallenberger, Noel Otto, Chuck Spalding, Emery Rubagenga, Andreea Bobis, Catalina Barbu, Dan Cantaragiu, Denisa Cantaragiu, Abdulaziz Alahmadi, Sulaiman Altehaini, Jassim Alharoon, David Covey (SMCov), and Minal Shah. Thank you to our children and grandchildren for letting us practice on you. The principles work!

To our amazing friends at Synergy Companies, you are among the best anywhere. To Dave Clark for being an incredible partner. His encouragement and support have influenced tens of thousands all over the world. And thanks to our great translation and feedback team: Miguel Becerril, Jose Montoya, Roberto Gonzalez, and the extraordinary leaders at Fundet/Funval.

To all of those not mentioned who have had an extraordinary impact on our lives: mentors, clients, friends, family members, and those who care. And, last but not least, to you who invest in this book and share this message with the world.

—STEVE

Introduction

William Shakespeare wisely said, "All the world's a stage, and all the men and women players; They have their exits and their entrances." Each one of us is a performer in some form or another and, as such, we will have our own entries and exits. Our promise is that this book will give you powerful tools to finally help you understand anxiety, work through it, and live life to its fullest.

Anxiety is something that will touch almost every life at some point.

As you read the following experiences of Brad, Liz, and Tom, see if you can relate to them in one way or another.

The applause in the auditorium started just as the sound of Brad's last note faded. He stood and made an obligatory bow. In shock and disbelief, he walked off the stage. He had never felt so awkward or embarrassed. "That was bad. They think I am an idiot. I can't believe I played like that!" Brad's post-performance self-bashing had begun. "I shouldn't have let Mr. Ramsey talk me into doing it. I should have said no. I didn't want to play in front of my friends. It was just a stupid awards assembly, but I have never been so nervous. I played it so well in practice—why couldn't I play it today? I'm never doing that again."

Liz was an aspiring, energetic sales manager who recently graduated from college. This was a new position and a new environment for Liz. Shortly after her first month on the job, the leadership team scheduled their quarterly meeting. They asked Liz to give a fifteen-minute presentation to update them on her sales goals and progress. Liz felt the all-too-familiar butterflies beginning to flutter in her stomach. She was great with people, but she was terrified of speaking in front of a group. As the meeting drew closer, she could barely sleep at night. Every time she thought about the presentation, her pulse quickened, her palms got clammy, and she became so anxious she couldn't focus on anything else. What would seem like a simple task to many quickly became all-consuming to Liz. She wondered how she could keep this job with this type of anxiety and stress. Should she quit and find something else? If she stayed, she knew she had to do something different to relieve this anxiety, but what?

Tom was a sophomore in high school and had decided to wrestle on the high school team. He had a good sophomore year and then trained throughout the entire summer while the other wrestlers were vacationing. Tom knew a family friend who happened to be the second-ranked collegiate wrestler in his weight division nationally. This friend, who lived only fifteen minutes from Tom, agreed to work with Tom one on one throughout the summer. By the time fall wrestling season came around, Tom was a totally different wrestler. At the beginning of his junior year, he wrestled one of the top wrestlers on the team (from the previous year) and pinned him in less than a minute. The coaches and other wrestlers immediately started to talk about how Tom would be the next state champion. Within a week of the spotlight being shifted to Tom, he started to have some strange thoughts and feelings he had never before experienced. He began asking himself, "What if I don't win the state championship and I let all these people down? What if I'm not as good as all the hype? Will I be a disappointment to my family and friends? What if I just quit? Would saying I could have been the state champion be better than trying and not actually winning?" The decision to continue or quit began to consume all his thoughts and energy. Practices became something he dreaded. He certainly wasn't prepared for these "crazy" thoughts and feelings, and he began to voice his concerns. The coaches pleaded with him not to throw away this talent. Other wrestlers tried to convince him to stay, but his anxiety and the fear of failure seemed too powerful, and Tom didn't know how to deal with what he was feeling.

Brad, Liz, and Tom were at a crossroads. They each had an important decision to make. Were they going to let anxiety rule them, or would they find a way to work through it and pursue their dreams? They may not have considered their decisions to be life altering in the moment, but how they handled those situations could impact the rest of their lives in at least two ways. First, they could change their direction, moving away from further skill development and all the experiences associated with it. Second, a pattern of avoidance would likely start or be reinforced, only to show up many more times in the future.

A lot of people can relate to Brad, Liz, and Tom in one form or another. Try to put yourself in their shoes and look for places past and present where you may have had a similar experience. It could be in any number of scenarios—during an athletic event, a talk you gave, acting, a performance, or a big presentation. Anxiety is a powerful emotion that is real and can have a big impact on a person's life. At times, this emotion is so strong it becomes debilitating. It's not uncommon for young men and women with many talents to change paths, throw away their careers, and struggle desperately because of their battle with anxiety. If decisions based on fear and anxiety aren't revisited and conquered, they become memories and, more than likely, bad memories. And when triggered once again, they can cause the same old fear and anxiety to show up in new, present-day situations. The patterns of fear, avoidance, embarrassment, and frustration only intensify the anxiety, which in turn decreases freedom.

Every time we face a fear, we grow and become more capable and confident. Every time we run from a fear, we lose confidence, the problem grows, and we feel more inadequate.

Brad, Liz, and Tom were in the process of developing their talents. But because they did not have the skills needed to deal with their traumatic experiences, they were stuck at a crossroads, no longer able to move forward on their own. Their feelings of anxiety were so overwhelming that avoidance seemed the only solution. Brad was no longer emotionally free or willing to play his cello and decided to forfeit his college scholarship. Tragic! Similarly, Tom gave up on his dream and his love of wrestling. Liz was on the verge of throwing away her new career.

As a psychologist, Jon hears lots of stories with the same unfortunate outcome. In addition, Rob and Steve, through Becoming Your Best Global Leadership, have trained hundreds of organizations around the world, helping them develop their people. All three of us frequently see instances where anxiety prevents people from trying something new, getting out of their comfort zones, or achieving their fullest potential. If a person doesn't learn how to conquer their anxiety, it can be with them for life. When we say, "conquer," we mean the ability to recognize anxiety for what it is, address it, and move forward towards a fulfilling and peaceful life. It doesn't mean you'll never feel anxious again or that anxiety will disappear, instead, you'll be armed with powerful tools to face it when it shows up in your life. This book will help you face it, because if you don't, what's the painful alternative?

For example, after one of our workshops, a woman in her seventies shared her painful story of a life full of performance anxiety. It all started at the age of sixteen, when she froze in the middle of her performance and forgot everything she'd played so well during her previous practices. She'd tried to restart, but she was so overwhelmed with anxiety and embarrassment she left the stage in tears. Over fifty years later, this experience *still* had a tangible negative influence in her life.

You've probably been able to relate to at least one of these stories in some way, or you certainly know someone who has experienced something similar. We understand that the journey to overcoming anxiety might feel difficult; however, given the skills you'll learn in this book, you will be able to address whatever comes your way.

While this book applies to everyone, you will see a lot of references to performance anxiety. As you consider the definition of a performer, think about the words of William Shakespeare once again: "All the world's a stage, and all the men and women players; They have their exits and their entrances." The truest definition of a performer in *Conquer Anxiety* is that we are all performers. The world is our stage. Whatever your interests, you're performing and sharing your talents, skills, or brand of leadership to improve the lives of others. Whether that performance is in the theatrical world, the world of business or music, in making a presentation, in selling a product or service, in sports, in the classroom, in your relationships, or in countless other ways, your success depends upon you giving your best performance possible while on that stage!

It is in that context that the ideas shared in this book, apply to you and each person as a performer.

There are a variety of lifestyle habits that reduce anxiety and stress such as quality sleep, effective time management, exercise, meditation and even professional services as needed for chronic anxiety. Having said that, this book is unique and there is nothing like it in the world when it comes to performance anxiety. The ideas in this book are founded on decades of research as to how to best conquer the anxiety that stands in your way. These powerful tools will help you become your best - to put on the best performance possible - so that when you finally make your exit, you feel wonderful and free.

No matter what level of anxiety you're dealing with, this book will help you find a way forward and break through the chains of anxiety so you can achieve your fullest potential. Part 1 focuses on helping you understand how the brain works and who you really are based on past experiences. To break free from anxiety and become a peak performer in any area of your life, you need to understand how your brain processes the performance experience. In part 2, you'll learn about the Five Stages of Peak Performance—a specific set of skills and techniques that will help you conquer your anxiety and optimize your performance. Once you understand how your brain works and apply the Five Stages of Peak Performance, you will be armed with a set of skills that enables you to finally break free of anxiety's viselike grip and to conquer whatever fears are holding you back. Whether you're a teenager or a seasoned adult, it's never too late to apply these life-changing tools. The Five Stages of Peak Performance provide a framework that shifts the context of a performance from "Practice and prepare really hard while fighting anxiety and the fear of failure" to "I know how to prepare, I know how to be ready to perform, I know how to bring my best when it counts, and I know how to learn from each performance."

The experiences of Brad, Liz, and Tom could easily be described as a normal, expected part of the learning curve. Unfortunately, because they didn't have the skills to deal with their fears, their experiences created serious negative emotions that could influence them for the rest of their lives. Given a mastery of the right mental skills, the same experiences could have become opportunities for growth. When performers of any age are trained in the Five Stages of Peak Performance and really understand the physiological and psychological responses we have to anxiety, roadblocks become stepping stones toward bigger and better things.

The Five Stages of Peak Performance methodology is the result of over thirty years of high-performance research, clinical practice, instruction at Brigham Young University, and experience gained from training and coaching thousands globally. Our goal is to share an approach that ensures the readiness of performers at any age or level to step out onto the stage of their choice, or into the public spotlight, and perform with confidence. Too many have developed the "safety at all costs" mindset which prevents them from sharing or doing the things they want to do. And that mindset works; it keeps them safe. But they don't perform, or if they do, it is more than stressful. You probably know someone who refuses to speak in public, share their talents, perform in front of people, or even try new things.

"At all costs" is a high price to pay. What you'll see in this book is that the Five Stages of Peak Performance can help you understand how to work through any anxiety you've experienced in the past so that you can feel bold and confident. Brad, Liz, and Tom didn't have the means to handle the challenging situations they faced. If they'd had the psychological skills and tools you'll learn about in this book, their initial responses would have been very different.

Without the mindset and skill set we need to conquer anxiety; we often find that both our personal and professional success later in life are negatively affected. In our training with various organizations around the world, it has been interesting to learn that nearly everyone faces anxiety to one degree or another (though many don't even realize it) and that, in most cases, the emotion is rooted in experiences of the past. That is why we've developed the Five Stages of Peak Performance. We believe they can help anyone optimize their performance. These powerful tools and techniques will help you discover how to move forward through the anxiety that, maybe in some cases, you didn't even realize was holding you back.

We are excited to help you conquer anxiety, optimize your performance, and live life to its fullest. For those reasons, this book is a beacon of hope to help you move forward with your life!

PART 1

CHAPTER 1
"I'm Activated"

(Please read the introduction before reading this chapter)

A studio full of young violin players was getting ready for the recital, the usual pre-performance excitement hanging in the air. Just moments before the recital was to start, Emma hesitantly approached her teacher. "I'm nervous," she said. There was a long pause as they looked at each other. Emma was silently saying "Help me, please," but it was obvious by the look of helplessness on the teacher's face that she didn't know what to say or do. Besides, the pressure to start the recital was mounting.

The silence was broken when the teacher tried to reassure her student with a weak, "It's all right. You will do fine." But Emma didn't feel at all reassured as she returned to her seat. When the recital started, her anxiety continued to build.

How would you have felt if you were Emma?

Have you ever felt anxious and wondered what you could do to calm your nerves?

Emma's story and those in the introduction had one thing in common. They lacked the knowledge and skills to use their brain as a peak performance tool. As Liz prepared for her sales presentation, she'd experienced something powerful and overwhelming, but the only way she could explain it at the time was with words like *anxious, nervous,* and *failure*. She didn't like what she felt and knew she was anxious, but she didn't understand what was happening to her mentally or physically, and, sadly, she didn't know what to do about it. In Brad's case, it was a no-pressure awards assembly, and yet he still felt humiliated—so humiliated he never wanted to perform again. Tom gave up his wrestling dream because he didn't know how to navigate his negative feelings.

The truth is that it wasn't their fault. They were never taught how to deal with their anxiety, and, consequently, had to rely on the only coping strategy they knew—avoidance! Emma recognized her need for help and asked for it, but she was turned away, empty-handed, to deal with her anxiety the best she knew how. This is a sad but very common reality for so many people.

Imagine for a moment that Emma's teacher had understood the cause of her performance anxiety and been able to proactively teach her students how to conquer it and mentally prepare for each performance.

We are confident that the brief conversation between Emma and her teacher would have sounded more like this:

Emma approached her teacher just before the recital was scheduled to start and quietly said, "I am nervous."

Her teacher responded with, "So, are you activated?"

"Yeah, I guess so."

"Of the performance tools we have been talking about in your lessons, which do you think would help you manage your activation?"

"The breathing exercises and mindset words."

"Which of the Five Stages of Peak Performance are you currently in?"

"Stage three."

"Right. It is time to get yourself mentally ready to perform. You have a couple minutes before it is your turn, so go practice the skills we've been learning. We will talk about how they worked at your next lesson. You've got this. It's time to start the recital."

A conversation of this nature would have made a world of difference for Emma. Think of the possibilities and doors that would have opened had Emma moved forward armed with this type of mental-skills toolbox. Unfortunately, what happened in real life was that her teacher basically told her, "Just suck it up. I can't help you."

Sound familiar?

We're going to talk about how you can conquer anxiety and optimize your performance. Are you wondering if you are part of the "performer" category? As mentioned in the introduction, "All the world's a stage, and all the men and women players." The truest definition of a performer according to *Conquer Anxiety* is that we are all performers. The world is our stage. Whatever your interests are, you're performing and sharing your talents and skills. That performance may show up in the theatrical world, in the world of business or music, in making a presentation, in selling a product or service, in sports, in the classroom, in your relationships, or in countless other ways. It is in this context that the Five Stages of Peak Performance apply to each of us as "performers." The powerful tools you're about to discover will help you put on the best performance possible, feel wonderful and free in the process, and become your best.

It all starts with your brain. For years, we have watched performers in all areas of life improve their performance when they start to look at their brain as a peak performance tool. Let's take a deeper look.

Brain Basics

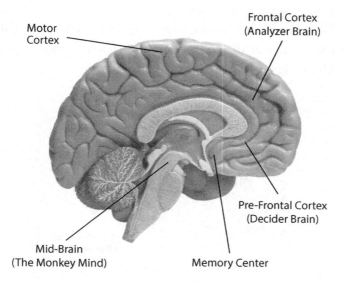

A performance of any kind (public speaking, sports, music, acting, etc.) involves many areas of the brain and body. When it comes to the expert performance of a learned behavior—such as speaking in front of a large group or shooting a foul shot on the basketball court—there are five areas of the brain you need to know about.

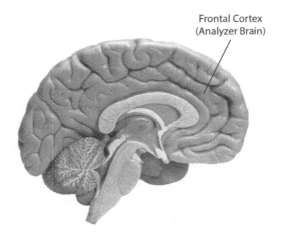

Frontal Cortex
(Analyzer Brain)

First is the frontal cortex. It's located just behind your forehead and is the largest part of your brain. It is responsible for analyzing information and it gives meaning to your experiences. This is the part of your brain that brings your knowledge together and allows you to be creative in all areas of your life. This is also where you use your values and goals to guide your actions.

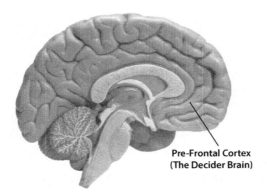

Pre-Frontal Cortex
(The Decider Brain)

Second is the pre-frontal cortex. This part of the brain is where decision making takes place. We like to call it the decider brain. It takes the information from the memory center, as well as new information from the five senses, and processes it all in the frontal cortex. From that information, a decision is made in the prefrontal cortex. You've heard the saying, "Think before you act." That saying refers to your prefrontal cortex.

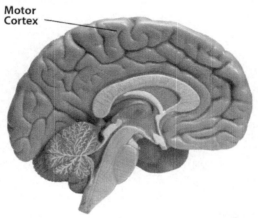

Motor Cortex

Third is the motor cortex. This part of the brain stores and co-ordinates all learned skills associated with movement. Motor skills are involved in every action we take, from drawing to catching a football. Motor skills also include something as simple as standing in front of a group of people

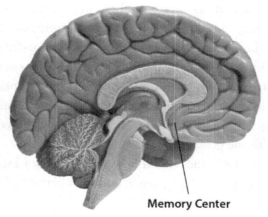

Memory Center

Fourth is the memory center. When a person practices and prepares for their next performance, their brain is storing all the important information related to that event in the memory center. What's stored in the memory center might include the words to a song, the sequence of a medical procedure, the next play in the game, or the notes to be played on an instrument.

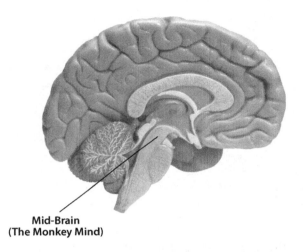

Mid-Brain
(The Monkey Mind)

Finally, there is the midbrain, which we like to refer to as the monkey mind. It is responsible for your emotions and, more specifically, it is the home of the amygdala or the stress response—fight, flight, or freeze (and lots of anxiety). The brain is so interconnected, it's not accurate to say that only these five areas are involved with a performance. However, it is important to note how the different parts of the brain interact to generate either peak performance or interference in the form of anxiety, distraction, or loss of confidence.

When it comes to executing a skill, everyone wants to perform well. We don't want anything, especially anxiety, to interfere with the message, story, information, or skills we've worked so hard to learn or with the goals we have set.

But if you don't understand how your brain works, you can experience feelings of anxiety, anger, and even betrayal. Oh, the pain, anguish, and frustration of, "I did it perfect when I practiced" only to "fail" onstage.

Stage fright, or performance anxiety, tends to get the most blame and attention, but we're going to pull back the curtain on what's really causing the anxiety. We're going to look at both the physiology *and* psychology of the anxiety.

The first thing you need to know about your brain is the relationship between the *voluntary* and the *involuntary* functions of the body. There are those behaviors that are under your direct influence and occur because you've made a choice. For example, when you go on a walk or sing your favorite song, those are under your voluntary control. There is also an involuntary system, which manages all of the things you don't control or consciously think about, such as heart rate, digestion, and blood pressure, to name a few. The involuntary system has two very important branches—the sympathetic and parasympathetic nervous systems.

Performance anxiety is the result of an involuntary activation of the sympathetic nervous system.

An activated sympathetic nervous system is often referred to as the "stress response," which automatically puts the body and brain into a state of fight, flight, or freeze. In our seminars, we encourage people to use the word *activated* rather than *stage fright, nervous,* or *anxiety* to describe any form of performance-related anxiety. You are not nervous, scared, panicked, terrified, or stricken with stage fright; you are simply "activated." From this point on, we will use the word *activated* in place of *anxious, nervous,* or *performance anxiety.*

To understand activation, you need to know about the physical and psychological symptoms behind it. It's also important to understand that this system is actually there to protect you. We learn about danger either through experience or through education. And whether through experience or education, once we learn something, our midbrain knows what to do and is ready to respond the next time we face the same danger. A conditioned response is in place, and when triggered, it automatically activates our stress response.

The stress response is perfect for the rare rattlesnake encounter on a mountain trail. If you've ever encountered a rattlesnake, you were probably grateful for the automatic response that helped you take the action you needed to be safe. It was the involuntary nervous system that was responsible for the initial response. You wouldn't voluntarily try to pet the rattlesnake because you know it could cause you harm. Often, even before you are fully aware of the danger, your brain and body have already reacted to the situation and the adrenaline (what we like to call "super juice") is flowing. The stress response is not activated by a request from your voluntary system. For example, you don't say, "Stress response, activate!" The stress response is activated by the involuntary system in reaction to something your brain perceives as dangerous.

Make a mental note: what your brain perceives as "dangerous" may not actually be dangerous. For example, are auditions, tryouts, or job interviews physically dangerous? Of course not. It's important to understand why the brain responds this way, whether the situation is actually dangerous or not.

Below are some important points to understand about your brain and your involuntary stress response:

- There are two small, pea-sized structures, one in each hemisphere of the brain, called the amygdala. They send the signal to your adrenal glands, which are on top of the kidneys, so that the super juice—adrenalin—starts flowing.
- The stress response is fully developed and functioning by the time a child is two years old, unlike the prefrontal cortex, which isn't fully developed until we are in our mid- to late twenties.
- Every signal, from every sensory nerve and the five senses, goes through the midbrain.
- Once the brain tags something as dangerous, either based on experience or education, it doesn't forget. For example, in the rattlesnake scenario, most people are afraid of rattlesnakes, and yet very few have ever been bitten or even seen

one in real life, but the education that rattlesnakes are dangerous is more than enough to trigger your stress response.

- The midbrain is like a radar, constantly scanning for danger. As soon as the radar picks up a blip or the buzz of a rattlesnake, that recognition is followed by activation.

- The stress response can activate faster than a heartbeat, yet it can take twenty minutes or more for the super juice (the adrenaline) to burn out of the system before you can fully calm down.

- When the stress response—the sympathetic nervous system—is activated, it suppresses the relaxation response, or the parasympathetic nervous system. The parasympathetic nervous system is the other part of the involuntary system that helps run your body automatically. This is important because the immune system is connected with the parasympathetic nervous system. Stress wreaks havoc on both the mind and body, in fact, you may have noticed that periods of high stress are often followed by an illness of some sort. This is one of the reasons why stress management and anxiety are important when talking about peak performance. Anxiety and stress influence both the sympathetic and parasympathetic nervous systems and can have a significant impact on your performance, health, and career.

- In its most basic purpose, the midbrain is tagged, or programmed, by the experience of some sort of physical pain. Yet it can very quickly link social and emotional pain with physical pain. And when the brain starts to link physical and social/emotional pain, when you learn you're wrong, make a mistake, or fall short of an expectation, it can trigger a stress response, even though there is no physical danger. This is what's at the root of performance anxiety.

- When the midbrain is activated, it quickly offers a first response that is manifested in behaviors and thoughts. Your first thought could be "I can't do that" because there are intense feelings of anxiety. Generally, performers shouldn't trust their first stress response. We'll explain why later.

- When your stress response is activated, it only has access to the part of the brain that is about fight, flight, or freeze, not what was memorized or prepared. This is why countless hours of practice can seemingly disappear and why your mind goes blank.

Are You Activated?

So, how do you know when your stress response has been activated? List five things that are likely to activate your stress response. What do you know makes you anxious?

1. _____

2. _____

3. _____

4. _____

5. _____

Think of the last time you found yourself anxious about something—a performance, speaking, hiking a steep mountain when you have a fear of heights, etc. It was obvious that you had a physical and emotional experience. Can you relate to any of the physical and emotional activation symptoms listed below?

- Tension, shakiness, or even tremors in your body
- Feeling like your heart is going to leap out of your chest
- Quick, shallow, rapid breathing, even hyperventilation
- Cold, clammy, sweaty hands caused by a decrease in circulation and an increase in perspiration
- Dry mouth
- Butterflies in your stomach

These are some of the more common physical symptoms a person can experience when activated. Let's get more specific and personal. It would be unusual if you experienced all of these symptoms at the same level of intensity. Different triggers will cause different levels of activation.

What are the physical symptoms you experience when your stress response is activated?

1. _____

2. _____

3. _____

4. _____

5. _____

Circle the symptom or symptoms that cause you the most difficulty.

For most, the physical symptoms of anxiety are easily identified. The psychological symptoms of anxiety are much less obvious. As we explore the psychological side of anxiety, you'll start to see that not all anxiety is triggered by a conditioned response. You'll recognize that what you think about a particular situation, performance, or event can often determine your level of anxiety. For example, in one workshop, participants took an assessment where they were asked some important questions to evaluate their psychological thought processes. One question asked them to complete the following sentence: *The audience is* _____. One response to this incomplete sentence was, "The audience is the enemy."

This performer had a powerful belief running in the background of every performance that generated interference and kept her from performing at her best. She felt her audience was the enemy. Because the audience was the enemy (in her brain), is it any surprise that she had extreme stage fright?

Here is a list of the mental/emotional symptoms indicating that your stress response has been activated.

- Distorted thinking
- Feeling overwhelmed or flooded with emotion
- Easily distracted
- Hyper focused
- Emotionally upset
- Avoidance or escape behaviors
- A loss of confidence
- Fear of embarrassment
- Loss of hope, vision, or possibility
- Fears and concerns for the future
- Shame, regret, or resentment for the past

It's important to understand how your mind and body work in conjunction. Think about familiar thoughts, attitudes, emotions, and behaviors you exhibit when you are stressed, or activated.

List the top five emotional or psychological symptoms you experience when you are activated (choose from the list above or write your own unique symptoms):

1.

2.

3.

4.

5.

Circle the symptom or symptoms that cause you the most difficulty. It's important to recognize these symptoms for what they are. We'll come back to them later in the book.

It is more than all right to run from danger. But running away from a goal, an opportunity, or even a "bad" experience is avoidance, and over time, that can be crippling. The power of—and the problem with—avoidance is how effective it is at deactivating the stress response. But it comes with a high price when a person sacrifices what could have been a great experience, a meaningful relationship, a dream fulfilled, or an important goal accomplished.

For example, Jim was a young man in the insurance industry who'd taken the test to become a broker three times. He needed a 60 percent to pass, but the last two times he took it, he got 59 percent. So close! He only needed to answer a couple more questions correctly and he would be a licensed broker. But his anxiety and feelings of failure kept him from studying and retaking the exam. When he came to see us, he wasn't planning on retaking the exam. Although he didn't realize it at the time, his anxiety was causing him to use avoidance as his primary approach, and it almost cost him his dream. He was introduced to the Five Stages of Peak Performance, discussed in Part Two of this book, and within a short time, he passed the test and became a broker. He just needed the right tools to move forward and to conquer his anxiety.

Sometimes anxiety is masked and can be very subtle. It may not even feel like anxiety, because we are often so good at avoiding the cause of the anxiety, we don't feel anxious. How do you know if you fall into this category? Phrases like "I don't want to" and "It's not my thing" may be a cover for underlying anxiety. This is what happened to Tom (the wrestler) in the introduction. Ironically, avoidance works! But, as we mentioned, there is a significant cost, and when avoidance is no longer possible, anxiety returns with a vengeance. Avoidance is a common and effective coping technique in dealing with something like rattlesnakes. The problem is when avoidance gets between you and your goals.

Let's talk more about how current beliefs and behaviors stem from previous experience and programming. In Jon's performance-psychology class, students participated in an experiment designed to be a metaphor for what happens during a performance. He took his class of musicians to a climbing gym. Everyone got just enough training to keep them safe, and within minutes the students were climbing the walls like a bunch of monkeys. It was obvious they were having a great time.

After some time, Jon noticed that one of the students—someone we'll call Susan—hadn't moved from the spot where they'd done the training. He approached her and asked if she planned to climb. She smiled and responded with "No, I'm too short." Surprised and perplexed by her response, he asked, "Where has being too short impacted you in the past?" She responded with a list that began with "I was too short to be the leading lady in the high school musical" and ended with "My hands are too small to play Rachmaninoff on the piano." She was then asked where she got the idea that she was too short climb in the gym. She pointed to the wall and stated, "You need to be five feet two inches or taller tall to climb here." There was a "5.2" on the wall, but what she didn't know was that it was a difficulty rating for the climbing route, not a height requirement (it really said 5.5, but the 5 was scratched and it looked like a 2). When she was informed that what she was looking at was a difficulty rating for the climbing route, she responded with an enthusiastic, "You mean I can climb here?" She enjoyed climbing for the rest of the evening.

This could be construed as a simple misunderstanding, but it is so much more. Susan had come to a new place for a new experience, yet something triggered her history of being too small, and she readily accepted the perceived height limitation.

There is nothing dangerous about a 5.2 on a wall, but Susan was trapped in a first response and didn't even know it. Something from her past jumped into her present and created what she thought was an appropriate course of action. We don't know where this belief came from, but it was there, and it had a big impact. The list of events impacted by her height was probably just the tip of the iceberg. Susan had learned to accept and be happy with her height limitations. When she saw a 5.2 on a wall in the climbing gym, she already knew exactly what it meant and was happy to accept that she was too short to participate. Because of her habitual first response, she no longer needed to evaluate the situation. She didn't know that climbing gyms don't have height requirements, she just assumed she knew what the numbers meant: "I am too short, and I'd better be happy about it." This was not a life-threatening situation, but her activated midbrain took control, and she followed an old, familiar pattern to safety—avoidance.

What type of mental programming may be negatively impacting you? We'll uncover some of those later in the book.

THE FRONTAL CORTEX AND PREFRONTAL CORTEX

To effectively deactivate the powerful effects of your stress response, you must engage your prefrontal cortex. We like to call the prefrontal cortex the "decider brain." Again, this is where decisions are made. It's where we make the decision to commit to a performance and to the process of what comes with that. The frontal cortex, or the analyzer brain, is where we pay attention to how we organize our time and schedule. This is where we compare what we do to what we expect. Part of this analysis is the determination of "Is this good enough or not?" It is in this part of the brain where we look at our performance expectations.

It is also important to see how essential engaging the decider brain is to deactivating the midbrain. In the instant that Liz realized her dread and anxiety got in her way, she felt helpless and didn't know how to move forward—she was activated. She didn't have the tools to conquer her anxiety, and the exit strategy of avoidance became more and more appealing.

In one workshop, we helped participants design the mindset they wanted to bring to their next performance. Students wrote three words on their name badges—bold, confident, and free. Then they were asked to really practice being bold, confident, and free for the next 30 minutes. Everyone was smiling and engaged—until we asked for volunteers. The room went silent. Eye contact was broken, and an awkward pause ensued. Everyone was overwhelmed by the response from their midbrain (flight or freeze), which was designed to keep them safe. Then a man near the front of the group looked at the positive trigger words on his name badge, took a deep breath, and said out loud, "I am bold." The initial request for volunteers had triggered a first response of "No," which came from the midbrain. Then, despite whatever level of activation this man experienced, his "decider" brain came online with the command to be bold, and he raised his hand to volunteer.

It is important to understand that the decider brain cannot override the physical activation initiated by the super juice of the midbrain. In other words, a person cannot deactivate the stress response simply by commanding it to deactivate. But when this student declared that he was bold and raised his hand, he was now moving toward, not away from, his vision to be a great performer. At this point, his anxiety started to decrease. He decided to accept the invitation to volunteer even though he was moderately activated. Because we cannot immediately deactivate our stress response, we tend to focus on our anxiety like it is something dangerous, and we become more anxious until fight, flight, or freeze takes over.

MEMORY CENTER

As one talented pianist entered the stage for her senior recital, she became highly activated. She was visibly shaking as she sat down, and the freeze response took over. Her mind went blank. It was like all her years of preparation were gone, nowhere to be found. Her worst nightmare had come true. She tried to compose herself. She even tried to play, but she was lost. She finally got up, walked off the stage, and didn't return.

She blamed her memory and what she thought was a memorization problem. Unfortunately, she didn't know that when her stress response was activated by a *real* or *perceived* danger, it had taken control of everything necessary to fight or run. When she was activated, you could say there was a figurative separation of her motor skills and the memory of her countless hours of practice. Why? Because her memory of the piano piece had no survival value, and her midbrain took over. Most of us can relate to this type of experience. Now you know why it happens.

Memorization is a skill, and there's a lot we can do to strengthen our memory and keep it sharp under pressure. But what we're suggesting is that, many times, it isn't a memorization issue; it's an activation issue. Activation is one of the primary reasons people seem to suddenly forget everything they know. Although the focus of this book isn't on memorization, there are some important basics we need to understand because they are a part of performance-anxiety issues:

- Memory is located in the hippocampus of the brain.
- The memory doesn't fill up like a hard drive; it always has room for more. That's why learning never stops.
- Memorization is a skill that improves with practice.
- Recently learned information is difficult to retrieve, and often feels like it is lost, when activation/anxiety is present.
- There are many tools and ideas to help with long-term storage and retrieval. Practice/repetition is the most frequently used strategy.
- Short-term memory is for those things that only need to be remembered for a few seconds. Your short-term memory is probably long enough to put someone's phone number in your phone.
- We remember long-term things for the rest of our lives. Examples might be riding a bicycle for the first time, your first address, and so on. Other things might need to be refreshed or we forget them. However, we learn them faster the second or third time because it's not like we are starting anew.

The memory part of the brain is important. That's why practice is critical to a great performance. However, if you're activated and are not able to access your memory, all the practice in the world is not going to help. That's why the tools in later chapters will become so important as you strive to conquer anxiety.

MOTOR CORTEX

The motor cortex is home to the physical skills needed to perform onstage, which are developed through practice. It doesn't matter if you are surgeon, a ballet dancer, or a basketball player, your motor cortex is the place where all of these intricate skills are stored.

In learning a new skill, we follow a very predictable pattern. Let's use juggling as an example. It doesn't matter what your starting point is. You may never have juggled, you may have tried it a few times, or you may know how to juggle well.

By the age of ten, most kids can toss a ball into the air and catch it with their other hand. In learning to juggle, we add new skills to what we already know. An interesting phenomenon happens here. When we add a new skill to an existing skill, there is often a breakdown in the old skill.

To learn the next skill in juggling requires us to really focus in order to create the new neural pathways necessary for the next step. We already have the skill to pass one ball to the other hand.

The next step is to learn the skill of timing so we can master the second step in juggling. The ball is tossed with the right hand, and just as it starts to descend, it is time to toss the ball in the left hand into the air. After launching the ball from the left hand, the ball from the right hand lands in the left, and the ball from the left lands in the right hand. Think of toss, toss, catch, catch.

The ball that was in the right hand is now in the left hand. This is challenging at first. The balls seem to be flying in every direction. It is often likely that previous attempts at juggling will access what we call the "toss/pass": one ball goes up, and the other ball is handed off to the left hand. We have seen a lot of frustrated people become surprised when they think the second ball will go up but instead gets passed to the other hand.

This is the power of old neural pathways. However, with practice and really focusing on toss, toss, catch, catch, they eventually figure it out and a new level of skill is developed. It is also interesting to note the neural pathways for the expletives often associated with frustration seem to emerge at this point. We have even seen people give up or lose interest. Avoidance is deeply ingrained in many of us.

With the introduction of a third ball or new step, what can we expect? Breakdown with what we've just mastered. Again, as the balls start to fly in every direction, there is the usual increase in frustration and the utterance of expletives. It can be quite humorous. At this point in the exercise, there is a new skill introduced. The next time we drop the ball, we shout, "Woohoo! I am learning to juggle." This is difficult because the expletive-of-choice response is difficult to change.

One of our coaching clients was an executive who was experiencing a lot of anxiety about giving the quarterly report to the board of directors. Juggling was part of his pre-performance training. A week later when asked about how his presentation went, he responded with a big smile and a "Woohoo! I am learning to juggle."

Let's simplify the juggling metaphor. The process starts with the focal point being a single ball. When you master one, you add another. When you master two, you add a third. When you can juggle with three, you are not really thinking about it. It just starts to flow. But anytime you add a new variable into the mix, you can expect a breakdown. So, if you added riding a unicycle while juggling three-balls, there would be various breakdowns in juggling and riding until a sufficient level of mastery emerged that allowed you to do both simultaneously.

Let's relate this to anxiety. Think about how frustrating it can be for a person to put in hours and hours of practice only to mess up during the actual performance. When a person walks onstage or into a performance arena, it introduces a new set of variables—the presence of an audience, holding a microphone, or dealing with an unexpected question. These new variables can interrupt the familiar neural pathways in the motor cortex, resulting in the possibility of performance breakdowns. Dress rehearsals and practice performances are a good way to address this. In athletics, we often refer to the "veteran factor." Veterans have more experience in the playoffs or the Superbowl. This is not a new environment for them, so less environmental interference is expected. They've got this!

When presented with a new task, you'll find that your focus starts out very narrow. However, with each step you master, you start to see the bigger picture—and soon you have the whole picture. The prefrontal cortex has to work less as you master your motor skills.

"Muscle memory" is the common term for the level of mastery where the muscles know what to do with little to no thought. There really isn't the capacity for memory within a muscle, but there is in the brain. Through practice and repetition, the impulses traveling along our neural pathways for a specific task become so efficient they actually use less energy, are faster, and the body seems to instinctively know what to do. This is where the memory center and the motor cortex connect and flow together. Anxiety interrupts or slows down this all-important connection. A very intentional focus is needed when we learn a new skill. When mastered, there is a lot less conscious attention needed to perform the task. The athlete who begins to overanalyze a well-practiced skill often creates mental interference that interrupts the flow. You may have heard the saying, "Paralysis by analysis." If the frontal cortex is trying to overanalyze what's going on, it can interfere with the free-flowing nature of the motor cortex. When the performer simply trusts himself or herself to perform, there is less observation and more involvement in the performance, which often activates the pleasure center. This is what we call "flow," or being "in the zone." We will talk more about being in the zone later.

The brain is a complex and amazing tool and knowing how the various parts of the brain work to support or interfere with your success is vital. Your performance history is important because guess where all your programming, or neural pathways, originated? Your history. Consequently, you have already developed neural pathways that promote and support a great performance, as well as neural pathways that get in the way and hinder progress. Because your history is so important when it comes to moving forward and conquering anxiety, we explore your history as it relates to experiences, beliefs, and attitudes in chapter two.

CHAPTER TWO
Your Background and History Assessment

Key to conquering anxiety is understanding yourself and why you get anxious (activated) in the first place. We've helped thousands of people conquer their anxiety and do the things they had previously given up on. One of the most important things you can do to move forward is to understand the past and what's causing you to experience these feelings and emotions; in other words, knowing what causes you to be activated. We've repeatedly used the brief assessment you'll find in this chapter and found that for it to be effective, you need to be honest with yourself when you answer the questions.

Once you've answered the questions in the assessment, we'll introduce the Five Stages of Peak Performance, to help you conquer your anxiety and move forward in life.

There are three reasons why it is important for you to actually answer these questions. First, there are different levels to the answers, and if you breeze through them, you will likely miss out on what you would have found had you dug deeper. Second, later in this book, you will be asked to reference your answers to specific questions, so you will only help yourself by investing the time now to answer them thoroughly and honestly. Finally, to really conquer anxiety, you need to get to the root cause of what's causing your anxiety and why you're being activated. These questions are designed to help you do exactly that.

That being said, let's get started on the questions!

Exercise 1

FOCUS AND EXPERIENCE

1. Identify three goals you have set for yourself that relate to you being a performer. These might include things like perform with the local symphony, be a starter on the high school basketball team, get a college scholarship, or give a talk in front of a group of people.

A.

B.

C.

2. What three dimensions of your experience as a performer would you like to see significant improvement in? This might include things like play a certain musical piece, perform with confidence, improve my speed as a runner, or talk without mumbling.

A.

B.

C.

3. If there were a dimension of your experience as a performer you could wave a magic wand over and just make disappear, what would it be (for example, stage fright or difficulty sleeping the night before, etc.)?

4. Write a description of your worst performance experience ever. Take a moment and let your mind wander, then find a "worst performance ever experience." It doesn't really matter what type of performance it was. If you labeled it as a worst performance, it has that meaning to you.

Write a brief description of it below:

Now, read the story you just wrote. Let's look at the emotional impact of this "worst performance ever." Find two or three words that describe or embody the emotional essence of this experience for you. For example, "I felt so_____," "I was_____," or "This was _____."

1. _____

2. _____

3. _____

5. Write a description of a personal peak performance (use as much detail as possible):

Now, read the peak performance story you just wrote. Find two or three words that describe or embody the emotional essence of this experience for you. For example, "I felt so_____," "I was_____," or "This was _____."

1.

2.

3.

Exercise 2

INTERNAL PROGRAMMING

The person you are today has been shaped by countless experiences. A child's journey is filled with discovery, attempts at mastery, and lots of good and bad experiences. The development of the child's brain starts out by relating to pleasure or pain. As the child grows and develops, the dichotomies of good and bad, success and failure, right and wrong, enough and not enough, rejection and being loved are just as big a part of the midbrain as the buzz of a rattlesnake or touching a hot stove. As we move through childhood, adolescence, and then on to adulthood, we hope to find the middle ground between the two extremes. However, we often have a lot of "all or nothing" reactions, even as adults. The following list of words will likely trigger an experience you had somewhere between your childhood and today.

To illustrate the power that certain experiences have had on your life, we invite you to look at each word on this list. When you read the word, think of an experience from your past that you can associate with that particular word. Then, write a brief description of that experience next to the word.

Success:

Fear:

Failure:

Embarrassment:

Disappointment:

Not good enough:

Love:

Validated:

Exercise 3

THE POSITIVE AND THE NEGATIVE

Identify three positive performance experiences and three negative experiences you have had. For example, the cello player we mentioned in the introduction would have listed his scholarship audition as a positive and his awards assembly performance as a negative. This will be important later in the book.

Positive:

1.

2.

3.

Negative:

1.

2.

3.

Exercise 4

THE SENTENCE-COMPLETION EXERCISE

Complete the following sentences. Just write whatever comes to mind. There are no right or wrong answers. Just finish the sentence.

____ 1. I get anxious when_____.

____ 2. Right before I perform, I feel_____.

____ 3. The worst thing that could happen during a performance is_____.

____ 4. After a performance I feel_____.

____ 5. I know I am ready to perform when_____.

____ 6. The audience_____.

____ 7. I feel satisfied with my performance when_____.

____ 8. Criticism is_____.

____ 9. What I like most about performing is_____.

____ 10. I get really mad when_____.

____ 11. Mistakes are_____.

____ 12. I'd have more confidence if_____.

____ 13. I get stressed out when_____.

____ 14. I am at my best when_____.

____ 15. I wish I could_____.

Consider that your answer to each of the above sentences tells a short but powerful story. Is it a positive story? Is it a negative story? Does this story support a great performance?

The next step with this exercise is to write a P for positive or an N for negative in the blank space in front of each sentence based upon whether you feel the statement was positive or negative. We'll explain why this is important later in the book.

Assessment Analysis

Now, let's look at Brad's assessment as an example of how you can use this to identify what might be preventing you from taking the next big step forward.

A SAMPLING OF BRAD'S ASSESSMENT
EXERCISE 1

1. What are your goals?
   To get a scholarship, play in college, and be a cello teacher.

2. In what dimension of who you are as a performer would you like to see significant progress?
   Coping with mistakes, confidence, and not having any stage fright.

3. If you could wave a magic wand over part of your performance experience and make it disappear, what would it be?
   No more stage fright!

4. Write down your worst performance ever.
   I was playing at a competition and forgot everything. I was so nervous. I wanted to run off the stage. I somehow started and played, but it was awful. I was so embarrassed.

5. Write three words to describe that experience.
   Embarrassing. Awful. Terrifying.

EXERCISE 3

Identify three positive and negative performance experiences.

Positive: I played well at my lesson last week. I got into the top high school orchestra. I loved the summer cello camp.

Negative: I didn't play well at the competition last year. I got really nervous and messed up when I was asked to play in class. I should have tried out for the salute-to-youth performance with the community orchestra, but I was too scared.

EXERCISE 4

_N_1. I get anxious when . . . *there are lots of people to play in front of.*

_N_3. The worst thing that could happen during a performance is . . . *making mistakes.*

_N_11. Mistakes are . . . *unbearable.*

_N_14. I am at my best when . . . *I am not nervous.*

_N_15. I wish I could . . . *play it perfect.*

When we examine Brad's answers, we can see that there are five negative attitudes or stories. These negative attitudes were a significant part of the emotional interference that contributed to not only his poor performance, but his decision to quit playing his cello.

What are the common themes in Brad's assessment? Embarrassment, anxiety, not meeting his expectations, and a huge fear of mistakes.

If you haven't already written your answers in the assessment, please pause here and do that - you will be glad you did.

Now that you have completed the assessment, go back and re-read your description of your worst performance ever found in question number four of exercise one. Also, re-read the three words you chose that embodied the essence of that experience.

Now, carefully read your answers on the sentence completion exercise and compare those answers to the words you used to describe your worst performance ever. Can you see similar attitudes in the other answers? Circle any answers that are even remotely similar to the words that you used to describe your worst performance ever.

Your answers tell an important story about you. They are likely to bring out the core themes, beliefs, and attitudes that make up the filter you are using to process your experiences. Most of these attitudes go way back into your past, but they are surfacing in your present and are likely to be what is getting in the way of you bringing your best to your performance.

Identify three to five "themes" that create the interference that gets in the way of you performing at your best. If you have difficulty identifying themes, find someone you trust and share your answers with them. The themes are there; it's just a matter of being able to see them. For example, a theme might be fear of failure or rejection. In Brad's assessment, his themes were perfectionism, fear of mistakes (failure), and being highly concerned about how others perceived him.

List the common themes that might be preventing you from achieving your best performance:

1.

2.

3.

4.

5.

Did Brad's "bad" performance cause the life-changing course correction that had him wanting to give up the cello? No. It wasn't his bad performance; it was his lack of knowledge; his lack of understanding of how the brain works, and his lack of the necessary skills to use his brain as a peak-performance tool.

We can only guess what Brad's future would be like today if six months prior to his awards assembly he had taken this assessment and applied the Five Stages of Peak Performance. Imagine if he would have also had coaching to help him conquer his performance anxiety, create reasonable expectations, and learn something from each performance. Unfortunately, Brad didn't have what you will have.

Reflecting on your own assessment, how can you relate to Brad, Liz, or Tom? Was there a time you either gave up or almost gave up something because of an unpleasant experience? Are you currently in a battle to stay the course or give up on something?

Now that you have a basic understanding of the brain as a peak performance tool and have completed the assessment, it is time to learn the important skills that will help you shift your mindset and free yourself from the ugly grip of anxiety. We'll approach this together through what we call the Five Stages of Peak Performance.

The *Five Stages of Peak Performance* are based on Jon's experience as a researcher, educator, psychologist, as well as Steve and Rob's diverse high-performance research and training around the world. What you'll learn in this book replaces the old mindset of "Practice a lot and hope for the best, while fearing the worst" with a process anyone can follow to transform their mindset, their performance, and their life.

The *Five Stages of Peak Performance* follows a logical sequence:

Stage I	VISION
Stage II	READY
Stage III	SET
Stage IV	GO
Stage V	EVALUATE

The Five Stages of Peak Performance have had a huge impact on people of all ages and stages. In addition, the concept reaches far beyond music, sports, etc. It can be applied when you have an important presentation or job interview, are taking the ACT or SAT, and so on. When applied, the Five Stages of Peak Performance are life-changing!

Jon starts his university class the same way each semester. He has the students share what they hope to get from the class. One year, a very talented pianist shared, "Performing is the cruelest form of torture." And she was serious! Her distress and fear were evident. She became activated during performances and didn't know what to do about it. She went on to explain how the fun was gone, the joy of performing had disappeared, and how performing was so stressful she was on the edge of quitting. It was just too painful to continue unless something changed.

Jon was excited. Unlike Brad, this student was in his class, and she was going to get the tools and skills that would allow her to keep moving forward. He was confident that her story would change by the end of the semester. About halfway through the class, she shared how much fun she had had with a recent master-class performance. She was smiling again. She now understood what activation was and she had applied specific tools to help her conquer her anxiety. She'd regained her confidence, her love of performing, and she was excited about the future. Prior to the class, she had all but lost her vision, but now it was back in focus. This is what can happen when someone develops the right mindset and applies the tools we'll discuss throughout the Five Stages of Peak Performance.

There are three promises associated with the Five Stages of Peak Performance:

- First, your willingness to perform and put yourself out there will increase.
- Second, the quality of your performance will increase.
- Finally, and most important, your enjoyment will increase.

As we've traveled the world training individuals and organizations, it's clear that anxiety impacts a lot of people! It's important to understand that anxiety can impact you regardless of age, gender, or occupation. Whether it's the ability to stand up in front of a group and give a presentation, make a sales visit to a client, talk to someone about a sensitive issue, or even getting on an airplane, anxiety's debilitating, viselike grip is real and potentially destructive. Now is the time. Let us help you learn to apply the tools, conquer anxiety, and get your life back!

PART 2

··

THE FIVE STAGES OF PEAK PERFORMANCE

CHAPTER 3
Stage I: Vision and Motivation

You may recall Liz from the introduction. She had just graduated from college and taken on the role of sales manager in a fast-growing organization. She was thrilled with this incredible job opportunity because it aligned so well with her strengths and vision. Yet, when the leaders of the company asked her to give a short presentation to the leadership team at their next quarterly meeting, everything changed.

Liz became activated!

Somewhere in her youth, Liz developed a deep fear of public speaking, and now she avoided it at all costs. Every time she thought about the presentation to the leadership team, she felt butterflies in her stomach, clammy hands, and an overall sense of dread. It wasn't long before she couldn't stand the thought of going to work because it meant she would have to think about the presentation. Her enthusiasm and love for her new career path were quickly fading. She became so anxious she was ready to quit her job, throw away this incredible opportunity, and choose a different career where she would never have to stand in front of a group.

Fortunately, at this critical juncture, she learned about the Five Stages of Peak Performance. Just understanding the word *activation* was a huge step in the right direction for Liz because now she had a way to understand what was happening and she knew what to do to manage this situation. After completing the same assessment you took in chapter two, Liz had an awakening as to why she felt the way she did. She had a context for how powerful her previous experiences were in shaping her life, her feelings, and even her thinking. She devoured information about the Five Stages and immediately applied the principles and tools. To her amazement, everything changed. She now understood that her presentation was actually a performance, and she realized its significance as a great opportunity in her life.

Her entire demeanor transformed after applying the Five Stages, she now felt excited about her presentation. When the time arrived, she was still activated, but her response was that of a peak performer: she acknowledged the activation and applied the tools she'd learned in the Five Stages. In the end, she gave a great presentation, and the president of the company complimented her on her presence, attitude, and ability to speak. She did it!

Prior to learning about activation and the Fives Stages, Liz was caught up in her midbrain. She had been focusing on all the things that might go wrong, and that negative thinking about the presentation was consuming her. To her credit, she applied what she learned, and it altered her course in life, helping her conquer something that had previously been debilitating. She found a renewed confidence, and what was previously a deep-held fear became something she looked forward to because she realized she was a pretty good speaker. What a transformation!

By this point, you surely want to get into the Five Stages and see how they can help you. So, let's get started!

Stage I: Vision and Motivation

Some time ago, Julie, a student in Jon's performance psychology course, met him after class and began to describe the anxiety and dread she was experiencing about her upcoming senior recital. She increasingly avoided practice and felt her motivation waning; she acknowledged that she had become debilitatingly anxious about the whole thing. There was a growing fear she would let a lot of people

down if she failed. Julie was working herself into a stressful performance experience. Jon applied the structure of the Five Stages to her
upcoming senior-recital experience by asking her three extremely
important questions:

- What is your vision or goal?
- What is your motivation for this performance?
- What is your current attitude or mindset about pursuing
  this goal?

When asked about her goal, Julie indicated that it was to pass
her senior recital. When asked to describe her motivation, she said,
"They are making me." When asked to describe her current attitude
about the upcoming recital, she exclaimed, "I am hating it."

No wonder she was stressed! Her answers to the three questions
were at the root of her anxiety. Thankfully, as she and Jon explored
her answers and the role they were playing in her experience, she
was able to break out of her stress-producing perspective and realign
herself with her true vision.

She realized that her senior recital was her choice. No one was
making her give a senior recital. When she'd chosen to get a degree
in music, she'd chosen a senior recital as part of that degree. She'd
known about the recital years in advance. When asked about why
she was pursuing a degree in music, she began to talk about her
love of music and the excitement she experienced when her students
progressed and learned new things. Once Julie reconnected with her
vision, or the source of motivation, behind her music degree and
senior recital, she began to have a sense of clarity and was able to see
the recital as a stepping-stone on the path to fulfilling that vision—
becoming a piano teacher who truly made a difference in the lives
of her students. As the foundation of her performance shifted away
from her anxiety and back to her vision (Stage I), the whole context
of the performance changed. What she had come to dread instead
became a fulfilling experience. In the end, she had a successful and
even enjoyable senior recital.

Your Vision

So often, it is easy to focus on the problem. What's wrong with that? It's the wrong place to start. Focusing on the problem can conjure up all-consuming negative emotions that suck away your energy and motivation. The good news is that your vision is a powerful tool to help you overcome this. A clear vision brings purpose, clarity, and gives you a direction. The vision is often a place of excitement, hope, and possibilities.

We've had the chance to train people all over the world and based on the extensive research we've done along the way, we've found that, surprisingly, only 1 to 3 percent of people have a written personal vision. This percentage transcends industry or age. Think of the ramifications!

Your vision is the seed of your legacy. When planted in fertile soil, a seed has a chance to grow. If the seed isn't planted, it doesn't even have a chance to grow. Imagine the power that flows into a person's life when they have a vision that is meaningful and provides clear direction. That person is so much more likely to stay focused because they have a *why* that becomes the source of energy they need to push through their current circumstances and stay on track. When we're knocked down or going through a challenge, which is likely to happen in the process of achieving a goal, it's a lot easier to get back up when we have a vision.

In the context of anxiety, it's easy to let the problem drive our feelings and emotions. Yet, when we step back and ask ourselves what our vision is, we put ourselves in the driver's seat, rather than the anxiety driving us.

This is a good time to talk about the difference between a vision and a goal. A vision is usually the why and is more long-term in nature. A goal is specific, measurable, and it's a milestone on the way to accomplish the vision.

For example, Julie's vision was to become the kind of music teacher who helped transform the lives of her students through music and life lessons—that was her *why* or her vision. A goal for Julie might have been to finish her senior recital by May 15 or to learn a certain technique or song by the end of the semester. Again, the vision is the why; the goals are the specific milestones that help you achieve that vision.

Many people start out with an ambitious and wonderful vision, but when they see their vision fade in the face of the struggles along the journey, they often become anxious, frustrated, angry, and even depressed. No fun! Julie was so focused on her fear of failing her senior recital, she lost sight of her vision. Julie knew she was off track but didn't know why or what to do about it. When she realigned her vision, goals, and attitude, everything changed.

Let's relate this to you.

Look at your day and the different roles and activities that are a part of your life. You probably have a wide array of performances, accomplishments, or things you want to do in the future—some small and some big. As you think about these performances, events, or things you want to do in the future, ask yourself *why* you want to do them. Think about that for a few minutes, write your answer below, and let that become your driver—your vision!

What is your vision (your why or purpose)?

Pause and reread the initial thoughts you came up with in describing your vision. If they give you meaning and direction, you've got it. If not, consider what's missing in your vision and put more thought into it.

Now, let's connect your goals to your vision.

As you think about your vision, or your why, what are some important goals and milestones that will help you achieve that vision? Fortunately, if you answered the questions in the earlier assessment, you already have a jump start on this. In exercise one of the assessment, you identified three goals as well as three dimensions of yourself you wanted to improve as a performer. Are those answers in line with your vision? It is important you have a specific performance, event, or thing you want to accomplish that aligns with your vision.

In this case, just pick one. The following questions will help you go a little deeper and build on what you already did in the assessment.

Ponder and write your answers to the following three questions:

What is your goal (it should support your vision)?

What is your motivation for achieving this goal?

What is your current attitude or mindset about pursuing this goal?

Have you written down the answers to these questions about your vision and goals? We will refer to them later in this chapter, and it's important to your success that you pause and actually write down your answers.

Even though most people haven't written out their vision or goals, many have at least thought about them. The ideas are in the brain—the intention is there—now it's a matter of articulating what that looks like. Any goal you have in mind should support and be in line with your vision.

As a reminder, your vision is your why, your purpose. The goals are the specific milestones or steps that bring your vision into reality. Considering what you just wrote, is your goal in line with your vision? Any thoughts about what things you might need to realign in your life to achieve your goal and vision? This is a great starting point on your journey to conquering your anxiety because you are now focused on your vision rather than on the problem.

Engaging in this simple activity in Stage I can bring a powerful shift in your life. You've just moved away from the problem and realigned your energy towards your vision. You've embarked on a journey that only 1 to 3 percent of the population will ever start! Once you've finished writing your vision and goals, put them where you will see them nearly every day. To make them even more real, consider sharing your vision and goals with key people in your life. You could share them with a family member, teacher, coworker, supervisor, or close friend. The accountability that comes with sharing your goals will help you stay focused on the achievement of your vision.

If you want to take a deeper dive into developing a personal vision, read our book *Becoming Your Best: The 12 Principles of Highly Successful Leaders*. It will help you with specific examples and ideas. Principle #2 in that book — Lead with a Vision — takes an in-depth look at the specifics of a personal vision.

Motivation

Once you've connected with your vision and the goals that support that vision, it's time to look at the second part of Stage I—your motivation. This is a close cousin to your vision. It's important to understand what really motivates you so that you stay focused on what you want to accomplish. When your vision is clearly defined, you should be able to answer the question of *why* you're doing what you're doing. There are likely a variety of reasons motivating you, but some reasons will be important and others less so. So far, you've identified and written down at least one of your goals. Now, as you think about that goal, come up with at least three reasons *why* you are pursuing that particular goal. This could be something as simple as "The boss asked me to make the presentation" or "I have always wanted to go to Machu Picchu to see the amazing ruins."

List three reasons why you are pursuing your goal:

1.

2.

3.

As you look at your list of reasons, one of the first things you'll need to do is determine the source of your drive—your motivation. Is it coming from you or an outside source? Sometimes you might even have a split, such as 70 percent from your boss and only 30 percent from you. External sources of motivation often fall into the categories of rewards and punishments. Internal sources of motivation tap into commitment, values, and passion. Although external motivation can be powerful, internal motivation is usually stronger and longer lasting. If everything you listed is externally motivated, you may want to consider determining what your internal motivation is. Doing so will help you achieve your vision and your goals because that motivation will be much higher and stronger since it comes from you.

We like to refer to the two types of motivation as the land of "I Choose" and the land of "Reasons Rule." Julie was clearly in the land of Reasons Rule. She was doing a senior recital because, she claimed, "They are making me." In the land of Reasons Rule (the world of external motivation), external reasons dictate what you will be doing and why. When Julie decided to get her degree, she was in the land of I Choose. But when the fear and anxiety began to build, she left the land of I Choose and entered the land of Reasons Rule. This was the source of her loss of power and motivation. When she became aware of where she was and made the choice to leave the land of Reasons Rule, stepping back into the land of I Choose, her perception of her senior recital changed: "It's my choice and part of my vision is to be a piano teacher who makes a difference in the lives of her students." She found a connection to sources of power that were bigger than her fears.

In the land of I Choose, a person takes ownership of their decisions and everything that comes with those decisions. If you choose a job as a manager after college graduation, you accept everything that comes with that decision: you may have to move, hire and fire people, give presentations, lead meetings, and so on. If you choose to pursue a sport as part of your vision, you accept everything that comes with that decision, such as conditioning, long hours of practice, possible injuries, and the thrill—or disappointment—of your fans.

Clear vision and goals from the land of I Choose are based on conscious choice. Your vision and goals should empower you; they should put you in a position of control. So, the next time you are tempted to complain or step into the negative about an upcoming performance, pause, breathe, and check to see if you've stepped into the land of Reasons Rule and are experiencing a loss of power as a result. Then, go back to your vision and the land of I Choose. For example, imagine the employee who resents the corporate decision of no time off for the next three months because it's the busy season. The employee previously made other plans during those three months, so now he needs to decide—should he follow through with his plans and lose his job or forgo his plans and stay employed? Assuming he decides to forgo his plans, he has the potential to feel frustrated and develop a negative attitude—which could poison his career. This is a scenario where he needs to make a conscious decision to go back to the land of I Choose and remember that this was the dream job he chose to pursue and that this is simply one of the things that comes with this particular job.

Whenever we set our sights on a goal, we need to choose an attitude that supports the achievement of that goal.

Most of us can relate to the excitement of a new goal. We can probably also relate to what happens two weeks later when the excitement wanes and the reality that the goal was much more challenging than we thought sets in—that's when the motivation can easily disappear. It's important to know what to do when your motivation diminishes, or your attitude takes a nosedive.

Take a moment and think of several words that describe the attitude you want to have when you perform. Don't choose vague, outcome words such as *great, perfect,* or *fantastic.* For a successful performance, you need to start by *being* the way you want to be. The doing follows naturally. Write three words that describe the way you want *to be* and the attitude you want *to have* when you perform. For example, you may wish to be bold, confident, and expressive. We refer to these words as "**trigger words**"—words that produce the mindset and attitude you are choosing to bring to your next performance. Whenever you feel yourself becoming activated, shifting to the negative, or losing motivation, your trigger words can bring you back to the vision and shift your entire mood. They can have a big impact on mood and motivation.

Here are some examples of trigger words:

Bold, confident, free, excited, inspirational, expressive, dynamic, sparkling, powerful, generous, flexible, willing, open, genuine, captivating, connected, playful, joyful, engaging.

By no means is this a complete list. You can experiment with a variety of words that work for you in different situations or different parts of your performance.

What is the attitude—use the trigger words that describe that attitude—you want to support your performance? Make sure you are using adjectives or trigger words that describe a *way of being,* such as *excited, sparkling,* and *aggressive* rather than a generalized outcome such as *perfect, great,* or *awesome.* Choose from the list above or come up with your own.

A. _____

B. _____

C. _____

This would be a good time to go back to the assessment in question five of exercise one. Look at the three words you used to describe the peak performance you wrote about and look for similarities to the answers you just came up with here.

Peak performers are aware of the importance of mindset and accordingly design a positive attitude that supports their entire performance experience. Let's summarize what you've done up to this point:

What goal did you come up with earlier in this chapter?

_____

What are the three trigger words you chose to support this goal:

1.   2.   3.

It's your responsibility to notice when your attitude is not in line with these goals and recommit to the positive trigger words whenever necessary.

A commitment to being positive is important because your attitude can shift at any point in the performance process. When there is a shift toward the negative, you must be aware of it so you can take charge and get back on track. The ideas you'll learn about in Stage II (the next chapter) will help you break through any negativity or activation you're feeling. The first, and sometimes most important, part is to notice the shift, then come back to the vision/goal so you can successfully apply the tools we'll talk about in Stage II.

Because it's important to know when your attitude is beginning to change, quickly write what signals or cues you recognize as red flags that indicate a negative shift in attitude or action (away from your trigger words)?

-
-
-

Once you recognize these signals or cues, the next step is to take action to make the shift from the negative back to the positive. Although you'll learn a lot of new ideas and tools in later chapters, let's talk about a few things you can do to improve your mood, motivation, and attitude. Examples could be a hike, meditation, a massage, a sporting event, reading, and so on.

What are the top three healthy activities you could engage in that will help you reset your mind and reconnect with your vision and goals?

1.

2.

3.

These are likely things you have tested in the past that helped you improve your attitude and mood. If they are healthy and uplifting activities, keep doing them! These activities coupled with what you're about to learn in the next several chapters will make a huge difference for you.

Conclusion

Mastering the tools and strategies you've learned about in Stage I is essential as you strive to conquer anxiety and achieve peak performance. Think about it. If you were to go right to Stage II and start applying the specific techniques that help with activation and stress, it would be like putting on a Band-Aid — you're helping with the symptoms but never addressing the real issue. This is why your vision and motivation are crucial in conquering anxiety. Knowing your why takes you to the right starting point and helps you shift from the problem (which can be all-consuming) to your vision.

Armed with your vision, goal(s), and the correct mindset, you're now ready to apply some new and powerful tools. With this mental preparation, you're ready to experience the amazing benefits that come from the techniques and ideas you're about to learn in Stage II.

STAGE I: VISION AND MOTIVATION
SUMMARY AND ACTION ITEMS

YOUR VISION

1. Shift from the problem to the vision.
   What is your vision (your why, or purpose)?

2. Develop a specific goal(s). These are milestones to help you achieve your vision.
   - *What is your vision or goal?*
   - *What is your motivation for pursuing this goal?*
   - *What is your current attitude or mindset about pursuing this goal?*

YOUR MOTIVATION

1. What are the three main reasons you are pursuing your goal? (Remember that internal motivation is usually stronger and longer lasting than external motivation.)

2. What are three trigger words that will support your goal(s) and shift your attitude, especially when you feel activated or are consumed in negative self-talk?

3. What are the top three healthy activities you could engage in that will help you reset your mind and reconnect with your vision and goals?

CHAPTER 4
Stage II: Ready (Mental and Physical Preparation)

Performers invest a lot of time and energy in developing their skill set. As you know, practice and repetition are essential to a great performance. But what about when you've put in the practice, mastered the skill, and done the work, yet you still become activated and have a breakdown because of interference from your brain?

This chapter will help you master the mental and physical skills you need to boldly move forward, address activation the right way, and confidently perform when the time arrives; hence why Stage II of the Five Stages of Peak Performance is titled "Ready." It's all about the physical and mental preparation it takes to be ready to perform at your best!

There are two primary parts to this chapter:

- The first covers techniques and exercises to help you be at the optimal level of *physiological* activation.
- The second focuses on the *psychological* part of activation and will help you psyche yourself up rather than psyche yourself out.

There are three skills top performers use to both mentally and physically prepare for an event. Skill #1 is primarily focused on *physiological* (physical) preparation, whereas Skills #2 and #3 are focused on *psychological* (mental) preparation:

- Skill #1 Activation (Anxiety) Management
- Skill #2 Positive Self-Talk
- Skill #3 Mindset Management

As you learn more about each of these skills, you will quickly see that there are a lot of strategies and tips to help you master each skill. Even though this is the longest chapter in the book, it will be one of the most life changing. You shouldn't feel overwhelmed by all the exercises in this chapter; rather, you should feel excited about *trying different ideas* to find out which works best for you. One practice that might be helpful is to bend down the corners of certain pages so you can come back to these techniques and exercises over and over again at your own pace.

To get you started, we've developed a simple assessment that gives you a chance to rate yourself in relation to each of these three skills and assess how you currently feel about yourself. Although we'll get into each of these in detail, here is a brief summary of what each skill means:

- *Activation (Anxiety) Management* refers to how well you manage the mental and physical experience of anxiety.
- *Positive Self-Talk* is the internal dialogue or the words you choose to describe your experience with a performance. The idea is to keep it positive.
- *Mindset Management* has to do with how intentional you are about creating and maintaining a positive performance mindset.

With that brief introduction, rate how well you're currently doing with each skill (1 is low, or weak; and 10 is high, or very strong):

	1	2	3	4	5	6	7	8	9	10
1. Activation (Anxiety) Management										
2. Positive Self-Talk										
3. Mindset Management										

There's no right or wrong here. This is just a snapshot of where you are *before* you apply the skills learned in this chapter. It's a good indicator of your strengths as well as the areas you could improve in. As you look at your assessment, consider that your lower scores are likely areas that generate more anxiety and interference in your life. Let's use your self-analysis as a starting point to see what kind of improvement you see after applying what you learn in this chapter.

How to Achieve an Optimal Level of *Physiological* Activation

During one of our workshops, an all-too-familiar story from a participant named Julie came up. She shared how she had tried that "relaxation stuff" and it didn't work. Being confident in the effectiveness of our tools, we listened and tried to gather the facts behind her concern and skepticism. She described being the *Salute to Youth* guest artist with a well-known symphony. She was backstage waiting to go on when she became highly activated. She panicked. Her pulse began to race, and fear of failure dominated her thoughts. She desperately tried to think of something that would help. Then she remembered a random presentation she had attended and something about a breathing exercise taught during that presentation. She attempted to use that breathing exercise, but her efforts to de-activate her stress response failed miserably. She battled her anxiety throughout the entire performance. And although she made it through, it was an agonizing experience.

At that point in her life, she had little knowledge of the physical and psychological causes of her anxiety (which we discussed in chapter 1). Tom, the wrestler mentioned in the introduction, had a similar experience. Both Tom and Julie had the physical ability and talent to perform at the highest level; they simply lacked the skills they needed to deal with what they were feeling. Both were unequipped to address their negative thoughts and anxiety. The first time Julie attempted any type of breathing exercise was during a fully activated stress response. She'd put in the time and was well prepared when it came to her musical piece, but she lacked the mental skills to manage the stress and anxiety that came with this prestigious opportunity. Not surprisingly, she felt like the breathing exercises didn't work. She had heard about a tool but never learned when and how to use it in the right way.

If Julie had taken the same assessment you just did prior to her performance with the symphony, it may have looked like this:

	1	2	3	4	5	6	7	8	9	10
1. Activation (Anxiety) Management		X								
2. Positive Self-Talk							X			
3. Mindset Management				X						

She would have known which areas to focus on and how to be mentally ready for her big event!

No matter your starting point, Stage II will arm you with a powerful set of ideas and tools so you can be ready and not have to experience what Julie or Tom did. Imagine how different Julie's experience would have been if she could have enjoyed the magic of the moment and basked in the spotlight rather than fight her way through it. That's exactly what could have happened had she used the skills you'll learn in Stage II. If you put in the practice, you will have the right tools—and know how to use them—to be physically and mentally ready.

Before we jump into the techniques that will help you succeed, pause and take a few deep breaths. Inhale slowly and deeply. Close your eyes and imagine how your life will change when you transform areas that need improvement into strengths. The next step is to learn these techniques and make them a part of your life. This is exciting. You are in control. You can do what it takes to conquer your anxiety and drive your future!

Skill #1: Activation (Anxiety) Management

One of the most important skills you can have—and certainly one of the main reasons you're reading this book—is the ability to conquer anxiety and achieve an optimal level of activation. Learning how to achieve an ideal level of activation is the primary part of your physiological preparation. Anxiety is often seen as the enemy and something to eliminate. But this perspective only generates more anxiety. Some level of activation is required for every task or performance you have been, or will be, a part of. The real problem occurs when you are in a state of overactivation, more commonly known as stage fright, performance anxiety, nervousness, or stress. The goal with activation is to know how to optimize your activation and keep it from being too high or low.

A voice teacher once asked us if we advocated relaxation strategies. Jon responded with an enthusiastic "Yes!" She then proclaimed that she would never refer her students to us because she didn't want them to be relaxed onstage. What this teacher didn't understand was that people simply need to know how to manage their level of activation as it relates to the task. Some situations require a high level of energy, while others need a much lower level. For example, in gymnastics, the floor exercise demands a very different level of energy than the match-winning putt for the professional golfer. For each task there is a window of physiological activation that supports a great performance. If you are either overactivated or underactivated, you are outside the window and will consequently deal with a lot of physiological interference.

Another example of this physiological interference was a basketball player who habitually threw up before every game because of "nerves," or at least that's what he believed it was. However, he was really just overactivated prior to the game and had no idea how to move his anxiety into the optimal range. His habitual routine didn't serve him because he lacked the skills to manage his activation.

Somewhere between too much activation and not enough is optimal activation. The diagram below describes the Activation Window, also known as the Yerkes Dodson Law. You perform your best when your level of activation is within this window. If your energy is too low, you will lack the drive that comes with a great performance.

If it is too high, you are likely to experience a breakdown in motor skills, memory, and concentration. It is all about learning to maintain an optimal level of activation for what you are doing.

Activation Window

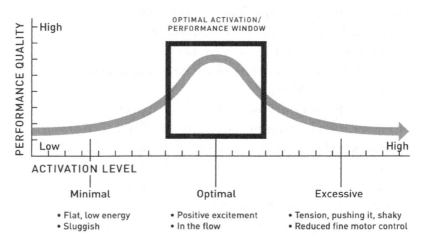

It's important to address underactivation, which is often related to issues like poor physical health, sleep deprivation, depression, lack of motivation, avoidance, and boredom. Many of the skills and tools we'll discuss related to overactivation will also make a positive difference for a person who is underactivated. However, the focus of this book is to help you manage overactivation (anxiety) and bring it into the optimal range. Skill #1, Anxiety Management, is focused on helping you manage overactivation by learning how to get into the optimal activation window.

There are three key areas in managing your stress and anxiety (overactivation). Each area consists of several simple, yet powerful, exercises and activities you can engage in to immediately initiate the deactivation process, which, in turn, will help you achieve an optimal level of activation.

There are three key areas that will help you master the skill of Anxiety Management:

1. Breathing

2. Mindfulness and Relaxation

3. Meditation

You will notice that there are numerous exercises and activities to choose from in each of these areas. You might wonder which exercise is the best or most effective. The answer is the one you practice!

Breathing

Breathing exercises are wonderful because they can help you calm down, relax, and minimize activation prior to a performance or during a stressful moment. What's great about these exercises is that they are simple and quick—they take only one to five minutes. The moment you feel the symptoms of overactivation coming on, you can use these breathing exercises with quick results. Because of their simplicity, most people don't practice them often enough to enjoy the benefits. Each time you practice a breathing exercise, you train your body to start the process of calming down on command. You can't control getting activated (the super juice), but you can use your decider brain to start deactivating. And with practice, your body will start to respond more quickly.

A breathing exercise has three parts:

1. Start any breathing exercise with a declaration of safety: "Body, it's safe. It's time to relax."

2. Unlock the diaphragm and breathe with your belly. When a person is activated, every muscle in the body tenses because of the super juice. The diaphragm, the muscle just beneath your lungs, becomes tense. You've probably heard the phrase "It took my breath away." What that is really describing is a frozen diaphragm, which makes it almost impossible to breathe. By intentionally breathing from your belly and unlocking your diaphragm, you enhance your body's ability to relax.

Before you start any breathing exercise, it's important to focus on belly breathing. If you are breathing with your diaphragm, you should see very little, if any, movement in the chest and shoulders. You should also be able to feel the stomach move away from the spine as you inhale and move toward the spine as you exhale.

Let's get a feel for belly breathing. Pause for a moment and pay attention to how you are breathing right now. Where do you see and feel movement? Try placing a hand on your belly. Is your hand moving gently away from your spine, then toward it?

To really get a feel for belly breathing, place your hand on your belly button while taking a big, deep breath, then loudly exhale, hissing until all the air is gone. While you're hissing, you should feel your hand move toward your spine. Next, inhale very slowly and pay attention to the middle of your body expanding. Your chest and shoulders do not need to move. It takes some practice to master belly breathing, but it is a component of almost every relaxation or meditation technique. Instead of "chest breathing," you want to get to the point where you are truly belly breathing. That will come as you use it in each of these exercises.

3. The third step is to choose a breathing exercise that will help you with anxiety management. Most of these simple exercises will only take about a minute or so.

BREATHING EXERCISE #1 (1–2 MINUTES): FIST SQUEEZE

Start with the declaration "Body, it's safe. It's time to relax." Begin to belly breathe. As you inhale, gently bring your hands into fists. Squeeze your fists tightly, and as you exhale, open your hands and say out loud, "Body, relax." Try this now. Do this exercise ten times and pay attention to the way you feel after just a few breaths. To do this exercise ten times should take less than a minute!

BREATHING EXERCISE #2 (1–3 MINUTES): FINGERTIP

Start with the declaration "Body, it's safe. It's time to relax." Begin to belly breathe. As you inhale, squeeze the fingertip of the little finger on your right hand with the thumb and index finger of your left hand. As you exhale, release the pressure on your fingertip and say out loud, "Body, relax." Go to the next finger, squeeze the fingertip, and as you exhale, say, "Body, relax." Continue to do the same thing with each finger until you finish that hand. Then switch hands. Repeat the process on the other hand, starting with the tip of the little finger. Do this until you have finished with all your fingers. This exercise creates a mental and physical focus on the pressure in the fingertip. It connects the breathing, the declaration of being safe, and the command to relax the body.

BREATHING EXERCISE #3 (1–5 MINUTES): PACED BREATHING

Start with the declaration "Body, it's safe. It's time to relax." Begin to belly breathe. As you inhale, count to four, and as you exhale, count to four. The goal is to keep the same pacing to your breaths in and out. This is particularly effective when you are breathing rapidly, and you want to intentionally slow your breathing. With practice, you should be able to inhale to the count of six, then exhale to the count of six. Some people find a slight variation of this exercise effective: inhale to the count of four, hold your breath for four counts, then exhale to the count of four and repeat. You can do this for a minute or until you feel your activation subsiding to a normal level.

BREATHING EXERCISE #4 (2–3 MINUTES): FIRE AND ICE

Start with the declaration "Body, it's safe. It's time to relax." Begin to belly breathe. As you inhale, tighten every muscle you can throughout your entire body— "ice up." Curl your toes, bring your hands into a fist, squeeze your arms into your sides, flex your legs, and tighten your core. Hold the tension while you count to ten, and then, as you exhale, completely relax your entire body, letting the ice melt away (fire). Then just breathe normally for three or four breaths and repeat fire and ice as many times as it is comfortable and effective. People of all ages love this one. Try this right now and see you feel.

BREATHING EXERCISE #5 (3–5 MINUTES): PROGRESSIVE MUSCLE RELAXATION[1]

Start with the declaration "Body, it's safe. It's time to relax." Begin to belly breathe. This may take a few minutes longer than the other exercises, maybe in the five-minute range. As you inhale, focus on the breath and talk to your body, part by part, while instructing it to relax. For example, inhale and say, "Face and neck, relax," then exhale. Deep breaths. "Shoulders, relax." Let your breathing relax. Let your core relax. Let your right leg relax. Let your left leg relax. Now, as you inhale, curl your toes. As you exhale, relax your toes. As you breathe in, push your heels into the floor. As you exhale, relax. As you inhale, tighten your core, then relax it as you breathe out. Bring your hands into a fist while you inhale and relax them as you exhale. As you inhale, bring your shoulders toward your ears, then relax them as you exhale. Repeat three to five times.

You could read this out loud, record it in your own voice, and then listen to it while following the instructions. Check out "progressive muscle relaxation" on the internet for more information.

BREATHING EXERCISE #6 (2–5 MINUTES): FULLNESS

Start with the declaration "Body, it's safe. It's time to relax." Begin to belly breathe. Start with any of the other breathing exercises, and when you finish, continue with this one. As you inhale, think the word *grateful*; as you exhale, say out loud, "full of gratitude." Repeat. As you inhale, think *grateful*; as you exhale, say, "full of gratitude." We call this the fullness breathing exercise. You can substitute the word *grateful* with words such as *hopeful, peaceful, beautiful, powerful, wonderful,* and *joyful.* You can also use some of the trigger words you chose in Stage I. Each of these words can help you direct your mind and body in a positive direction while you focus on your breathing. From earlier chapters, you've learned that words like *stressful, fearful,* and *resentful* can actually create stress. At the opposite end of the spectrum, positive words can defuse stress and help deactivate the body. Even at this moment, notice how your body responds to thinking "grateful" as you inhale and "full of gratitude" as you exhale. Do this for ten to twenty breaths.

These few, simple breathing exercises can be used to effectively manage (decrease) anxiety when you want to deactivate or when you're feeling stressed. Consider folding the corner of these pages down so that you can come back to them again and again. If you haven't practiced the breathing exercises, we highly recommend you do so now, so that you've practiced them at least once.

To really enjoy their powerful benefits, we invite you to start doing at least three breathing exercises a day. They could last between one to five minutes (or more if you desire). You will be surprised by what you notice as you bring these powerful exercises into your day. It's amazing how simple and effective they can be if you practice them. You will get the most benefit by making them a part of your daily routine rather than using them only when you're feeling activated or stressed.

The next part of managing activation is learning to be mindful and to relax so you can come back to the optimal level of activation.

Mindfulness and Relaxation

Mindfulness starts with an awareness of what is in your mind. It's like asking the questions: What are my thoughts? Am I choosing what is in my mind? Is my mind full of things that generate peace and confidence or stress and anxiety? Being mindful is when you intentionally call into your mind those thoughts that support your goals and vision. Below are six exercises that can help you be mindful, or present. By making these a part of your daily routine, you proactively manage your activation and/or stress so they stay at an optimal level. In many cases, simply becoming aware of a negative mindset and taking immediate action can diffuse overactivation before it ever happens. Each of these simple exercises can be done in five minutes or less.

MINDFULNESS EXERCISE #1: STICKY NOTES

Write "Pause, breathe, relax" on three separate sticky notes and put them in a place where you can see them often. As you see them throughout the day, pause and breathe—just like we discussed in belly breathing. Notice a coolness as you breathe in and a warmth as you breathe out; tell the body to relax.

MINDFULNESS EXERCISE #2: RING TONE

Set a ring tone on your phone that will go off three times during the day. Consider it a call to do one of the breathing exercises as soon as it's convenient. Even if you're not in a position to do one of the breathing exercises when the phone goes off, pause and breathe for a few seconds or pause to focus on your current thoughts and feelings. The idea is to be mindful of the present and replace any negative thoughts with peaceful, confident, and positive thoughts.

MINDFULNESS EXERCISE #3: STOPLIGHT

The next time you are at a stoplight, declare that you are safe, keep your eyes open, and notice your breathing. As you inhale, squeeze the steering wheel, and as you exhale, loosen your grip. Keep doing this until the light turns green, then proceed calmly. Stay aware of your surroundings and don't do anything you wouldn't normally do while driving. Recently, one stressed-out mother reported that she was at her wits end while taking her kids to soccer practice. She pulled up to a stoplight and tried this exercise, and, to her amazement, when the light turned green, she felt the stress melt away and a sense of control flow into her soul. She was surprised at how quickly her mood shifted when she used this exercise.

MINDFULNESS EXERCISE #4: WALKING WORDS

As you are walking from your car to your office or a store, do a walking word recitation. Alternate the words *grateful* and *peaceful* with every step. As simple as this might sound, think about what it's doing to the brain. How can the brain focus on anything negative or stressful when you're saying these types of words with every step? You can use any of the positive trigger words you came up with in the previous chapter. For example, how would you feel if you walked from your office or workplace to an important supervisor meeting saying *bold* and *confident* with each step?

MINDFULNESS EXERCISE #5: BE PRESENT

Mindfulness is about being present, so pause and listen for three things you can hear (birds, insects, etc.). Look around and identify five things in your line of sight (trees, flowers, etc.). Look at the horizon or at the farthest thing away from you and simply notice all the things you can see as you bring your focus to where you are in the present moment. What do you smell? What do you feel? Notice the texture of your clothing or the temperature in the room. Sometimes just focusing on the present can help a person relax.

MINDFULNESS EXERCISE #6: TAPPING

Tapping, or what some call the Emotional Freedom Technique,[2] is an exercise that can help bring your awareness to the present while reducing anxiety. Practice tapping to proactively manage your anxiety, especially when you're feeling activated.

There are nine points on the body you can gently tap to stimulate the nerves and help relax the body. Gentle tapping helps you become mindful of the present so you can get out of your own head. This can be especially helpful in starting the deactivation process.

Below is a description of where you can locate the tapping points:

1. The soft flesh on either hand between the little finger and the wrist.

2. The eyebrow bone directly above the pupil of the eye.
3. The eye-socket bone near the outside corner of the eye.
4. The cheekbone directly below the eye.
5. Between the nose and upper lip.
6. Between the lower lip and chin.
7. Where the collarbone joins the sternum.
8. About four inches below the armpit.
9. The crown of the head.

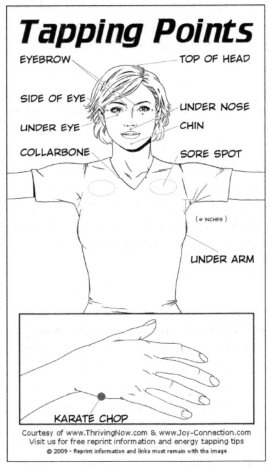

Tapping Points

EYEBROW — TOP OF HEAD

SIDE OF EYE

UNDER NOSE

UNDER EYE — CHIN

COLLARBONE — SORE SPOT

(4 INCHES)

UNDER ARM

KARATE CHOP

Courtesy of www.ThrivingNow.com & www.Joy-Connection.com
Visit us for free reprint information and energy tapping tips
© 2009 · Reprint information and links must remain with the image

Start the tapping exercise with "Body it's safe. It's time to relax and reset." Begin to belly breathe, then start with tapping point number one. Some people like to begin tapping with the phrase "Even though I am experiencing (state your concern), I love and accept myself and (state an affirmation about the problems or concern)." For example, "Even though I am experiencing a lot of stress about my upcoming presentation, I love and accept myself, and I can see myself making this presentation with confidence and ease." This is said while tapping each point. As you practice, you will find what is most comfortable and what works best for you. Tapping is very forgiving, so don't worry about tapping the exact right spot or getting the words exactly right—anything you do will be helpful.

The most basic form of tapping is to simply tap on each point while you inhale and exhale. Then, with the next breath, go to the next point. You may want to take three to five deep breaths per point. Once you have gone through the tapping points to relax and reset, you can go through the sequence again with a positive affirmation. Try the tapping sequence with affirmations such as "I am capable," "I am prepared," "I am bold and confident," and "I can manage this with confidence and ease." Later in this chapter, you'll see how important self-talk and affirmations are to psychological well-being.

Meditation

Meditation can consist of a single breath, a prolonged walk, or sitting for hours, but the benefits of meditation can be experienced in just a few minutes and can have a profound effect on your physical and emotional well-being[3]. The only way to know how meditation can affect your life is to do it. Yoda, from the blockbuster movie Star Wars, wisely counseled, "Do or do not; there is no try." Meditation is one of those things that we should all be doing, not just thinking about.

The good news is you don't need to study with a Yogi in India or a monk in Tibet to learn how to meditate effectively. You do not have to sit in what looks like an uncomfortable position for hours to call it meditation. All you need to do is establish a specific time where you focus on calming your mind and relaxing your body.

If this is your first attempt at meditation, you will quickly discover how difficult it is to really focus on the actual meditation experience. You'll find that your mind tends to naturally wander all over the universe. This is okay. Don't worry about it; you are just learning. As you begin meditating, we recommend you start out as an observer of your experience. What are you aware of? Every time you redirect your thoughts to what feels important, you are starting the process of becoming the master of your thoughts. In the beginning, notice where your thoughts tend to go and then refocus on your breathing. For example, you want to relax, but thoughts about a project at work keep entering your mind. It can be helpful to say something like "I will have all the time I need to work on that project after I have finished my meditation" or "Right now my priority is meditating." When you exhale, say "Body relax" as you notice the air leaving your lungs. Sometimes just repeating the words "In-breath, out-breath" gets you refocused. Some people worry about falling asleep during meditation. If that happens, great (assuming you're not sitting in your work chair). If you fall asleep, it's because you need it!

Another recommendation to help you meditate effectively is to listen to audio of a meditation session. Visit www.AnxietyConquer.com, where you'll find several great exercises ranging from three to thirty minutes and free video and audio downloads that will help with meditation and the other exercises so that you can refocus, deactivate, and get back to the optimal activation level. If you're asked for a code on the website, use the code *deactivate* to get free access.

Here are a few quick guidelines to help make your meditation more effective:

- Find a comfortable, safe, calm place. You can sit, stand, or lie down. Find a place where you won't be interrupted during your meditation.
- Start with the declaration that you are safe and that it is time to relax.
- You may want to set an alarm if you are concerned about falling asleep. As a reminder, if you fall asleep, it simply means your body needs the sleep.

- Schedule a regular time so that you are at a reduced stress level when you meditate. The more you meditate and practice these exercises when you are not stressed, the more effective they will be when you are stressed.

- Get in the habit of doing a relaxation exercise as you fall asleep at night. It can dramatically improve the quality of your sleep. Try it tonight. As your head lands on the pillow, bring your attention to your breathing. As you exhale, think *sleepy* and *tired*, then tell your eyes and forehead to relax and follow the routine for the progressive muscle relaxation exercise from earlier in this chapter.

- As you begin the day, take a few minutes to meditate and focus on positive affirmations. We call this a "Becoming Your Best Morning." It helps you align with your vision, see what success looks like for that day, and start the day with a victory. Whatever happens, don't check your phone first thing in the morning. For additional examples of what you can do and include in a Becoming Your Best morning, visit www.AnxietyConquer.com.

- When you feel yourself getting activated, give your symptoms a rating between zero (no anxiety) and ten (debilitating anxiety). It is important to recognize that not all activation is equal. Then start your breathing exercises, mindfulness exercises, or meditation. When you finish, rate your symptoms again. You will typically experience a drop of two to five points, which translates to a feeling of peace and control. It also means you will go from being overactivated to getting back into the optimal activation zone, which is powerful!

Important Note: While these exercises and techniques will help with almost any type of activation, when people report an activation level of nine or ten, it is likely they are moving out of performance-related activation and into a clinical level of anxiety. Panic attacks, phobias, and generalized anxiety are best addressed by someone who specializes in anxiety disorders. If you feel yourself moving toward an activation level of nine or ten, please find a good psychologist who can help provide treatments specific to your situation in addition to everything you'll learn in this book.

Each of the exercises we've talked about (Breathing, Mindfulness, and Meditation) will help you manage your anxiety, which is the first skill to master while preparing for an event. What did you notice when you tried these anxiety-management exercises? Was there one that really seemed to work for you? Experiment with the breathing and mindfulness exercises and you'll discover which are most effective for you. There isn't a right or wrong way to do these, so don't get anxious about getting it exactly right. The more you practice the exercises, the better you'll feel. If you need to slightly modify them to work for you, then do it. For example, one client modified the clench-the-fists exercise and turned it into a curl-the-toes exercise, which was more conducive to his business meeting in the board room, where he was trying to deal with the anxiety he was experiencing.

You might be wondering how to incorporate breathing exercises or meditation into the actual performance experience. That will come later in this book. Right now, you're developing the skill of "on command" relaxation through breathing and mindfulness exercises as well as through meditation. Mastering this skill—Activation Management—is the first of three skills in Stage II that will help you conquer anxiety and optimize your performance.

The power of all these exercises is in the practice and daily use. The benefits of these breathing, mindfulness, and meditation exercises are huge when it comes to activation management. They have been well researched by countless experts, and they work! Now, time for you to do your personal research and see what kind of results you get. We are extremely confident you will benefit from your experience. Make the commitment now to do at least three breathing exercises a day for an entire week. At the end of the week, evaluate your progress with your ability to control your activation.

Skills to Address Psychological Activation

One important function of the brain is to give meaning to each experience we have. On a fundamental level, this is about survival. It's the midbrain's job to put everything we encounter into the categories of friend or foe, safe or dangerous, pleasure or pain. That doesn't mean it always attaches the correct meaning to an experience but meaning is attributed to whatever we experience. This is exactly what happened to the student at the climbing gym. The 5.2 on the wall triggered feelings based on her previous experience, and she responded accordingly. She saw the 5.2 as a height requirement, and she knew exactly what that meant for her: she was too short to participate, and she was "happy" to be watching the other students climb. She didn't know that her incorrect thinking, not the number on the wall, was the problem.

The first skill in Stage II pertained to the physiological side of deactivation. The other two skills we'll talk about focus on the psychological side of deactivation. These skills are key in your preparation and can help you recognize distortions in your thinking that could be significantly contributing to your anxiety and challenges.

Skill #2: Positive Self-Talk

During a workshop in San Jose, California, participants were given a questionnaire and asked to identify their positive and/or negative attitudes as they related to their performances. One participant submitted her questionnaire with half of the questions left blank. Curious as to why she had left so many questions blank, we asked her if she wanted to answer the remaining questions.

She confidently declared, "No, thanks. I don't do negative." What an amazing answer!

Every question that drew upon a negative was left blank. "The scariest thing about performing is_____" was left blank. Somewhere during her life, she'd learned the power and importance of words and was unwilling to entertain the negative, even the hypothetical negative. It was obvious in her demeanor that she was a quiet, yet confident young lady. We can all take a lesson from this young performer. What if success and happiness were as simple as thinking happy thoughts? Amazingly, it oftentimes is!

Ralph Waldo Emmerson wisely said, "Sow a thought and you reap an action; sow an act and you reap a habit; sow a habit and you reap a character; sow a character and you reap a destiny." Our destiny is simply the fruit of our thoughts. Positive thoughts are the seeds of success. They eventually blossom and grow into massive trees. Negative thoughts are also seeds; hence why we need to be so careful which seeds we decide to plant.

How many successful people do you know who talk about failure all day long? They don't. It all starts with thoughts. For example, a marriage or relationship that includes a mentality ratio of five positives to one negative generally thrives and succeeds. PhD psychologist and relationship expert Jon Gottman found that when that ratio drops to one positive to one negative or less, the relationship is in serious trouble[4]. In other words, it's not a one-to-one ratio that predicts success.

Thoughts and words are similar. For most, increasing the ratio of positive to negative thoughts and reprogramming the brain takes significant effort. According to Dr. Helmstetter, in his book *What to Say When You Talk to Your Self*, the average person has been told *no* or what they *can't* do more than 148,000 times by the time they're eighteen years old.[5] That may be a contributing factor as to why 70 percent of our thoughts as adults tend to be negative.

It is easy to see how our words and thoughts either work for us, or against us, especially in preparation for an event.

In earlier chapters, you read about the physiological responses caused by the flood of super juice. You might also remember that there are psychological responses. Often, these physical and emotional responses happen so fast we think of them as the same experience, but there is an important distinction. While a person may have an automatic, conditioned response triggered by a stimulus, such as a rattlesnake, there can also be a triggered response to something not inherently dangerous or even close to life-threatening, such as an audition or job interview. Since there is nothing associated with the audition or job interview that is truly dangerous to a person's survival, it's the negative self-talk, or the internal story being told, that can trigger the stress response.

Creating the habit of positive self-talk is a critical skill because where your words go, you go!

We've found that many people fundamentally believe this to be true but aren't sure how to adjust their thinking. We'll share several strategies to help you start and/or develop positive self-talk and bring your thoughts and words in line with your vision, goals, and actions.

POSITIVE SELF-TALK STRATEGY #1: RECOGNIZE THE MONKEY CHATTER!

Monkey chatter cannot be trusted! We'll explain.

As discussed in chapter 1, negative thoughts come from the mid-brain and are usually triggered by something in the present—such as dropping a pass, not getting a promotion, or just making a simple mistake—that is related in some way to a past experience. Monkey chatter, from the monkey mind, is a metaphor that has long been used to describe the flood of negative thoughts that interferes with the creative, rational part of your brain.

As we searched for pictures that represented monkey chatter, the only images we could find seemed to be of smiling monkeys. Then the picture below popped up. Although we liked the energy in the monkey's face, we didn't want a monkey in a cage, so we continued the search. When we couldn't find any other pictures that worked, we took a close look at this picture, and as we did so, an interesting thought came to mind: "Who said the monkey was in a cage?" "Do we know the monkey is in a cage?" "No. It all depends on perspective!" It was at this point we decided it was the perfect picture to describe monkey chatter. Monkey chatter can become a cage made up of our very own thoughts and words. Maybe you can relate to this image in some way. Have you ever caught yourself thinking or say-ing the words "I can't do that," "I'm not enough," "I'm so stupid," "I fail at that every time," "Why even try?" or "Don't volunteer"? What if that was all just monkey chatter?

The next time you hear a troop of chattering monkey's screaming inside your head, pause and take a breath. It's just monkey chatter from the midbrain, and it can't be trusted! Don't listen to it. It's time to look for the second or third responses originating from your prefrontal cortex.

This is like the word *activated*. Wasn't it nice to have a name you could pin on your anxiety and stress? Like *activation, monkey chatter* is simply a name for these crazy initial thoughts that pop into the mind. When a person accepts that thoughts can be filled with errors, lies, and distortions—labeling them as monkey chatter is a powerful step to freeing ourselves from being trapped in our own minds.

POSITIVE SELF-TALK STRATEGY #2: THINKING ERRORS

The field of cognitive psychology is founded on the premise that our distress is often caused by the errors in our thoughts and words[6].

So, when people can recognize and change their thinking errors, they are better able to manage the situation, and their distress is consequently reduced. By changing a single word, a seemingly terrible situation changes into a difficult situation or even a manageable situation.

The following is a list of "red-flag" words or thinking errors that should raise a warning whenever you say, think, or even hear them. When these monkey-chatter words show up, they are likely to generate a lot of negativity, resentment, and anxiety. It can be surprising how often these categories of words or the words themselves show up in our vocabulary:

ALL OR NOTHING: Words like *always, every time,* and *never.* The absolute nature of these words creates an extreme perspective that is rarely accurate. But the tension, stress, and anxiety they create is very real. These all-or-nothing-type words are the source of a lot of defensiveness and reactive behavior, especially in relationships. For example, "*All* you do is sit on that couch" or "You *never* help out around here." Get ready for a fight. This is why we should generally avoid all-or-nothing words.

LABELS: Words like *idiot, stupid, worthless, failure, not good enough,* and *bad* create a limit on how people look at themselves or their situations. For example: "I am not smart enough to be a manager, so I am not even going to apply." The impact of labeling others, things, circumstances, or even yourself can last a lifetime if left unchallenged.

WOULDA, COULDA, SHOULDA: The words *would, could,* and *should* give power to someone or something else—they disempower you! In the past tense, they become like a club we beat ourselves over the head with: "I should have gotten that promotion," "I should have prepared better," "We should have won." In the future tense, they create anxiety and fear related to the expectation of an outcome: "I should be able to complete it on time." They can also be the source of a handy excuse: "I could do that if I had time. Sorry."

JUMPING TO CONCLUSIONS: It's easy to jump to a conclusion about what we think another person might be thinking or some future outcome. We then tend to act in accordance with those thoughts: For example, "He is not interested, so I won't even talk to him." Or, "I am not good enough to get a scholarship, so I won't even try."

MAGNIFICATION OR MINIMIZATION: We tend to blow things way out of proportion, or on the other end of the spectrum, we shrink their importance. For example, "My mistake ruined the entire performance."

Maybe you can relate to the first-response monkey chatter of a young man at a solo competition who forgot the words to his song. His immediate response was to angrily slap his forehead and shout, "Stupid idiot!" Let's take his unintentionally powerful statement "stupid idiot" and analyze it. This was his initial response, which we now know cannot be trusted. There could be many different reasons for his breakdown, but none of them confirms that he is indeed a stupid idiot. This is likely a conditioned response, a habit he's developed when things don't go right. It's the monkey chatter from his midbrain that came out of his mouth.

Now that you can recognize the monkey chatter in your thoughts and words, do you want to continue using the same old words and thoughts and creating the same outcomes? No!

Let's talk about how to tame the monkey mind and change the self-talk (chatter) to something that helps you move toward your vision and toward becoming your best. We'll use the "stupid idiot" example, but if you can think of something negative you've recently said to yourself, feel free to use that.

1. Recognize the negative thought: "Stupid idiot!"
2. Ask the two big questions:

> Question 1: Is it true or false? Am I truly a stupid idiot? *False*
> Question 2: What is the truth? *I need more than a day to memorize a song. It was going pretty well until I forgot where I was.*

Now, flip back to exercise two in chapter two. Look at the eight words (fear, validated, etc.) and their accompanying story. Choose one of the stories that illustrates an obvious thinking error and write a summary of that story below:

As you reread each sentence, ask the three big questions:

1. Is it true or false?
2. Are there any thinking errors, like labeling, in the sentence?
3. What is the truth?

Write the truth on the line below.

_____

When you write the truth, you challenge the monkey chatter and prove it false. When you practice stating the truth, you are charting a new course that will move you forward. If you're not sure what the truth is, share what you think it may be with someone else. Sometimes it's easy to get stuck in a proverbial monkey-chatter cage. It is empowering to challenge the chatter and break through to your truth. Monkeys live in the monkey mind or midbrain; the real you lives in your prefrontal cortex.

The sentence-completion exercise from chapter two becomes an important and powerful part of this strategy. Go back to that exercise and look at each sentence you identified as negative. It will be a huge benefit to you to look at each sentence and identify what is false and then state the truth. It may take some time, but you will be glad you did it. If you want to take this to the next level, consider sharing it with a trusted friend, coach, or mentor. "My first response to the sentence was _____, and the truth is_____."

The goal is to practice challenging the monkey chatter when it shows up and immediately replace it with the truth.

POSITIVE SELF-TALK STRATEGY #3: AND

When you recognize a negative first response (which can be a thought or statement), you can quickly redirect things by intentionally saying "and" after that negative response. Brad, the cello player, got stuck in the abyss of "I am not doing that again!" And that was the end of his story. There was no *and*. The next time you get stuck in the abyss, try putting *and* at the end of five thoughts or sentences. It will help shift you in a positive direction. Let's look at how *and* would have made a difference for Brad.

I am not doing that again . . .

    and it was embarrassing,

    and I got really nervous,

    and I didn't know what to do about all that anxiety,

    and I need to learn how to cope with getting anxious,

    and I am grateful I didn't play like that during my scholarship audition.

And now Brad has the words in place to help him move forward and to learn from his embarrassing performance. He will learn how to conquer his performance anxiety, and he will do it with a scholarship.

POSITIVE SELF-TALK STRATEGY #4: POSITIVE AFFIRMATION

This strategy will improve every aspect of your life when used correctly. The battle between positive and negative thinking goes back to the midbrain and the impact of remembering something perceived as dangerous to us. It is generally accepted that the human brain remembers the negative more readily than the positive. This also holds true with our self-talk. It takes a lot of awareness and practice to recognize old, dysfunctional thinking and intentionally replace it with something positive.

The use of positive affirmations is the practice of using specific words to create a positive belief around whatever you are doing. There are lots of different approaches, from making a list of things you are grateful for to practicing specific phrases, such as "I am well prepared," "I've got this," and "I can share my ideas with confidence and ease."

There's an old saying that goes, "Whether you think you can or can't, you're probably right." That's similar to Proverbs 23:7: "As a man thinketh, so is he." Both statements are true in a much deeper sense than we realize. There is a new and fascinating field of research that focuses on the brain. A new term that has become popular in recent years as a result of that research is *neuroplasticity*. The term refers to the plasticity of the brain; in other words, the brain is ever-changing, and we can literally rewire our brain. Since thoughts, self-talk, and our choice of words fire the neuropathways of the brain, we want the old negative self-talk to fade as we create new, powerful, positive self-talk. This certainly doesn't happen by accident. You can and need to teach your "old brain" new tricks.

Again, go back and look at your assessment in chapter two. When you look at your goals, as well as your positive and negative beliefs, you'll find a gold mine of information to help you customize affirmations that are helpful to you.

Let's use Brad's assessment from chapter two to customize an affirmation that works for him. While we look at his example, be thinking about your assessment and what affirmations might apply to you. Using Brad's responses from the sentence-completion exercise in chapter two, we've created three examples of positive affirmations. Keep in mind, there are a lot of variations; these are just a few examples:

1. I get anxious when *there are lots of people to play in front of.*
   - The people in the audience are my friends.
   - I am comfortable and confident in front of my audience.
   - What I am sharing is more important than how many people are in the audience.

11. Mistakes are *unbearable.*

- My preparation is complete, I can handle whatever shows up, and I will learn from every performance.
- The more mistakes I make, the faster I am going to learn what I need to learn.
- Mistakes are part of growth, and I learn from each one!

14. I am at my best when I am not nervous.

- I can use my excitement to bring my best to each performance.
- I feel calm and in control during performances.
- My message is what's important; people want this message because it will help them get better.

Review the negative responses in your sentence-completion exercise in chapter two. Find three negative sentences you came up with and develop positive affirmations to address each negative sentence or thought.

Negative sentence:

_____

Positive Affirmation:

1.

2.

3.

Negative sentence:

_____

Positive Affirmation:

1.

2.

3.

Negative sentence:

_____

Positive Affirmation:

1.

2.

3.

There are many ways to use positive affirmations. What's important is that you start using them to replace old, negative thoughts with new, empowering thoughts. Don't be surprised if stating an affirmation triggers a lot of monkey chatter. You have been in the habit of listening to the chatter, and now you want to challenge that chatter. Each time you challenge the monkey chatter, you are rewiring your brain, thanks to neuroplasticity.

Affirmations are also a good way to vocalize what you really desire. Our friend Thomas Blackwell wisely said, "What we talk about we bring about!"[7] Your thoughts and words are the captain of your ship. Once the captain speaks, the crew (your body and everything around you) goes to work to fulfill the command of the captain. When you choose to have an empowering internal conversation, you set up the type of thinking that lets you make the right kinds of changes in your life. You'll notice that when you speak positive affirmations, like those above, your posture and expression will change. You'll sit up straighter in your chair, your chin will come up, your frown or the creases in your forehead will go away, and so on. These affirmations come with positive mental *and* physical side effects!

These affirmations change the internal dialogue from monkey chatter to something that moves you in the right direction. For example, the negative thought "I'll never be able to make this presentation" can be turned into the positive affirmation "I present with confidence and ease." This affirmation helps you create a realistic vision of what you want your presentation to look like.

Some people experience resistance to positive affirmations because they think it is silly. Others find that affirming a new possibility can be overwhelming because it is so contrary to their familiar, negative way of thinking. Others may feel they are setting themselves up for failure again (that is a negative affirmation in and of itself). If you're skeptical about or resistant to positive affirmations, think about how that resistance might be used to reinforce the monkey chatter.

Monkey chatter can get loud. Monkey chatter would say it sounds too good to be true, so it must be wrong, or a delusion, and it might only work for a few select people. To the monkey mind, the affirmation "I can perform with confidence and ease" sounds as plausible as "I can jump across the Grand Canyon." For some, the affirmation may feel impossible in the beginning; it might even trigger a stress response. But when you recognize that all the opposing chatter is coming from the midbrain, your positive affirmations can move the discussion to the decider brain and quiet the monkey chatter.

Remember, you're rewiring your brain. It may not feel natural or even believable at first, but over time you are literally changing your brain.

Pause and breathe. What are some other areas of your life that would benefit from a change in thinking through using positive affirmations?

1. _____

2. _____

3. _____

As you've probably already figured out, while thinking about other areas of your life, positive affirmations can apply to much more than a single performance; it can apply to *every* area of your life. A few simple examples of more general affirmations are:

> *Everything always works out for my good.* (If we believe it, it becomes a reality.)
> *Today will be a great day!*
> *I am a finisher.*
> *I feel* <u>(insert desired positive affirmation)</u>; *I am* <u>(insert desired positive affirmation)</u>; *I choose* <u>(insert desired positive affirmation).</u>
> *Just realize that positive affirmations can transform your entire pattern of thinking, both as it relates to a specific performance and in life.*

Here are some ideas to help reinforce your positive affirmations so they become a permanent part of your belief system:

1. Print them out and put them in a place where you will see them often—the bathroom mirror, next to the bed, somewhere in your car, on your computer, and so on.
2. Write them in the morning as part of journaling your progress. As you write them, it will reinforce them more than just reading or saying them.
3. Combine your affirmations and your vision. Memorize that and repeat it each day.
4. Share them with a trusted friend or family member. There is great power in sharing something with someone else. It gets it in the open and enlists another person's support.
5. Create a symbol that represents the vision or affirmations and have it where you can see it as a reminder of what you believe is possible. It can be a necklace, ring, and so on.
6. Make your affirmations part of your screen saver.

7. Repeat your affirmations at the beginning of the day and at the end of the day. In many cases, we recommend saying them out loud at least twenty times a day—remember neuroplasticity.
8. Set an alarm on your phone with your written affirmation. Every time the alarm sounds, your affirmation pops up.

Skill #3: Mindset Management

Years ago, we led a workshop where a young man we will call Scott was in attendance. It was as if a toxic cloud surrounded him as he came into the room. He sat alone. He looked angry and unhappy. Years prior, he was diagnosed with a challenging form of cancer. After three years of treatments, he was finally declared cancer free. Since he had been through a life-changing and difficult experience while he battled cancer, his mom wanted to help him have a "normal" teenage experience and also have fun—hence why he was at this conference.

But the reality was that Scott did not want to be there. Later that day, in private, there was a brief conversation where he was asked, "Scott, what is your mindset about being here?" He responded with a terse, "This is lame. I want to go home." We then asked him, if he could grab the "This is lame. I want to go home" mindset, pull it out of his head, and throw it in the trash, what could he replace it with? A pause was followed by a hesitant "This is fun." The conversation ended with "Scott, you know your mom is not going to take you home and that you'll be at this conference for the next several days. So, you have an opportunity to make a choice. You can continue to hate being here, or you can manage your mindset." Two days later, there was a call from a grateful mom. She shared that Scott had begun to practice managing his mindset and that he'd had a total change in attitude. Scott was now excited to be there and was enjoying the conference. The unhappy-camper cloud was gone!

It has been said that if you don't manage your mindset, your mindset will manage you. Mindset matters because it determines what you see and what you are likely to do next. If your mindset is that this is going to be a stressful or boring meeting, it is going to be a stressful or boring meeting. Learning to manage your mindset is an important skill in Stage II as you prepare for your event or experience.

The brain, once again, is at the basis of mindset. The midbrain is the home of the default mindset—a mindset based on past experiences and part of the default first response. Your default mindset is just waiting for the right time to show up. Have you ever been in a group where someone asks for volunteers? Most of the time, a small number of people feel all right about volunteering, while most hesitate and wait to see what happens. And then there are those who never volunteer.

Monkey chatter and your default mindset are best friends. The call for volunteers is like a cue for the monkeys to start chattering, and you now have plenty of reasons not to volunteer. Once you become aware of the power your default mindset has, you will see just how much control it wields—its goal is to keep you safe no matter what. For performers, however, it cannot be trusted any more than the initial monkey-chatter response. It may not always be wrong, but when you recognize that a first response is taking you away from your goal and needs to be challenged, the decider brain can take over and realign with your goals. In the previous story, Scott engaged the decider brain and realigned his mindset.

Designing an optimal performance mindset (mindset management) is a skill that requires practice. The second and most challenging part of mindset management is to stay in it, to hold on to it, and when it shifts, to remain calm. The key is to refocus and get right back into your optimal performance mindset.

Jon and a colleague at Brigham Young University, Dr. Paul Broomhead, collaborated on two separate research projects[8] that explored the importance and power of mindset management. In two different studies, one with a college population the other with a teenage population, they were able to demonstrate how designing a mindset had a significant positive result on quality and self-expression during a performance.

They took 150 junior high choir students and asked them to go into a practice room with a video camera, where they were given the following instructions: "Sing 'Happy Birthday' as musically as you can." The students followed the instructions, and when they left, they were randomly assigned to return to the choir and to either be in the control group or the treatment group. After a forty-minute clinic with the treatment group on how to design a bold, confident, free mindset, all 150 students were asked to return to the practice room with the same instruction: "Sing 'Happy Birthday' as musically as you can." What the research clearly showed was that the forty minutes of instruction on how to design an optimal performance mindset had a significant positive result. In both the college-student and teenage-student populations, the treatment groups performed the second song with a statistically higher level of musicality, energy, and creativity, whereas the control group—the group that didn't get any additional instruction—had no real change in the way they sang the song.

Then, two weeks later, they were retested. Once more, the control groups did not change. However, there was one important difference in the treatment group when they sang the song a third time. The college population maintained the positive difference. The junior high students dropped back to match the control group. They had lost their edge. As we explored this difference, we concluded that, for a variety of reasons, the teenage population needed more practice. The whole point is that given the right skills and training, a person can literally create an optimal performance mindset. The other primary observation was that when it comes to mindset, it's not a one and done. Managing your mindset is an ongoing process.

We've trained tens of thousands of people around the world, and it's always interesting to watch those who are engaged and apply the tools. These participants will send an email two or three months after the training and talk about how their life has changed as a result of what they've learned. They're happier, more confident, their relationships have improved, and so on. When a person uses the tools and applies the principles we've talked about, their mindset begins to shift. It's easier to manage your mindset when you're doing the right things. That's why these Five Stages are each so important in the process. You'll find additional advice on developing a positive mindset in our other book, *Becoming Your Best: The 12 Principles of Highly Successful Leaders.* The habits discussed in both books will help you create and sustain a mindset by design and experience the transformation that follows.

In Stage I of the Five Stages of Peak Performance, you'll remember that we talked about motivation. Motivation and mindset are close cousins. This is something that will play a role throughout all Five Stages. It is likely that during the coming weeks and months, you will at some point experience a shift in mindset. Sometimes it can feel like an emotional roller coaster or even a love-hate relationship. How a person copes with these shifts is what is important—especially in preparation for a performance.

Jon once coached a collegiate softball player who came to see him because she'd recognized a mindset shift that was interfering with her game. She played third base, and while she was on the field, she prayed that the opposing team would not hit a grounder anywhere near her. This was a totally different mindset than she'd had her entire life, and she wasn't sure what was happening. Her aggressive, confident, and intense mindset had shifted to a fearful, don't-hit-it-to-me mindset. She was given the assignment to practice mindset management during her next practice.

She designed an aggressive, intense, and confident mindset and was ready for infield practice. And it worked; she was having a great experience. She felt good, was playing well, and her confidence had returned—until the coach shouted, "Have you had enough?" and her first thought was *Yes, I hate grounders!* Recognizing her shift back into a less-than-optimal mindset, she shouted back, "No, hit me ten more." This was a victory. She'd originally scheduled an appointment with Jon because she thought she was afraid of grounders. What she realized was that her shift in mindset was at the root of her anxiety, and as soon as she practiced intentional mindset management, she was back in the game.

Designing your optimal performance mindset is the easier part. Staying in it is the challenge.

Think back to a positive past performance. You may want to go back to chapter two and look at what you wrote in exercise one on the assessment. Focus on what you did great. Dig into the background and explore how you were *being* at that moment. What was your attitude like? How did you feel physically? What was your mindset? Write down three words that describe how you were being during that performance.

1. _____

2. _____

3. _____

These may be similar to the trigger words you came up with in Stage I. If so, great! If you were focused on the way you felt during that great performance or on the way you were *being*, you wouldn't be using outcome-focused words such as *perfect, flawless,* or *awesome.* Rather, they would be positive attitude words like bold, confident, and free—words that are positive-attitude focused.

When asked why we choose words like *bold, confident,* and *free,* we offer a fairly easy explanation. Being bold is stepping up, putting yourself out there. Confident is knowing you can handle whatever shows up. Too often *confidence* gets defined as "I know I will make the shot, get the job, or satisfy everyone." This may be part of psyching yourself up, but it is usually followed by a huge letdown if you don't achieve what you've set out to do. What a roller coaster ride! It doesn't take too many "downs" before getting off the roller coaster starts to sound like a good thing. *Free* means being free to play, to share, and to learn all you can from the experience. That word also signifies the freedom to succeed and to fail. You can probably feel why these powerful trigger words can help manage mindset.

Your trigger words should become important to you!

Any thoughts of victory or defeat can take you out of the high-performance mindset. For example, there was a viola player in Chicago who, when he played well, played very well. However, when he made any type of mistake, it started an avalanche of frustration, distraction, and things usually ended poorly. We asked him to come up with a couple of words he could use to anchor his attention on the moment and direct him toward the type of experience he wanted to have. His response was simple. "All I want to do is cope." *Cope* became his trigger word. He was instructed to recognize that anytime his attention was off target, he was to take a breath and say the word cope as a tool to help him redirect his attention to what was most important.

He came back a week later and was excited to share his experience. He was preparing to play a small solo as a member of an orchestra. His mute was on his music stand. With his bow in hand, he reached for his mute, but his bow touched his music stand, which quickly spun around and launched his mute into a crack in the floor. The mute was gone. There was a quick negative first response, followed by a breath, and then he thought of the word *cope*. In the mindset of *cope*, he noticed a mute on the stand of the person sitting next to him. He reached over and borrowed it. As he attempted to put it on his viola, he realized he'd never seen a mute like this before, and he couldn't figure out how to use it.

Again, he found himself breathing and saying the word *cope* as he handed his viola and the mute to its owner. She placed it on his viola for him; he was now ready to start his solo. Whereas a glitch like this would normally have thrown him off, he'd handled it with poise and confidence. This was one of two situations that came up during his performance. He was thrilled with how he now felt he could handle whatever came up.

So, what happens when the mindset shifts back to the negative or things don't go your way? When that happens, it can feel difficult to get out of that slump and shift back to the positive. Although there are a lot of factors involved, you can use the following six suggestions when you find your negative mindset managing you:

1. Acknowledge the shift into a negative mindset, then pause and breathe. Check the monkey chatter. Implement some of the exercises and strategies from the previous two skills in this chapter. Often, becoming mindful is all that is needed to refocus and reconnect with your predesigned optimal performance mindset.

2. Find a pen and paper to write about what you are experiencing. Write out the story so that you can see the facts and the meaning you give those facts. Then you can identify the meaning, the cost, and what you might be getting from your negative response. Just seeing it on paper can help clear distorted thinking.

3. Find the thinking errors (from earlier in the positive self-talk section) and apply them to what you are saying or thinking. Remember, *all-or-nothing, always, should, never, exaggerations, mind reading,* and so on. With the thinking error removed, you can now put together the kinds of words that will move you forward.

4. Do one of the breathing, mindfulness, or meditation exercises you learned earlier in Stage II. When you take time to calm your body, it allows the thinking part of your brain to come back online. Then you can look at the situation and mindset through refreshed eyes.

5. Talk to someone you trust. This could be a friend or a professional. Maybe you just need someone to listen as you vent or rant. An alternative is to focus on your intention to get out of the negative energy and back into your optimal performance mindset. This usually requires dropping an unmet expectation.

6. One final thing you can do to manage your mindset, especially as it relates to performance, is to practice with distractions. Let's talk about why this one is so important to mindset management.

During almost any performance, things that weren't planned for will happen, and you need to be able to roll with them. For example, Olympic swim coaches will purposely rip the goggles off a swimmer halfway through practice so that the swimmer is forced to swim with no goggles. If a wide receiver feels like they must have their gloves to catch, they can practice what happens if they lose a glove and are forced to play with only one. How about if you're playing the piano and someone starts coughing or one of the keys suddenly doesn't work? We give keynote talks and workshop presentations all over the world; you can bet we've practiced what we would do if the computer were to suddenly crash.

There are a million scenarios; the point is that you want to create a focused mindset so that if or when something happens, you're not mentally thrown off by it. And that all starts with preparation and practice. Purposely create distractions in your practice and preparation and your confidence will soar. Then, if something happens during the performance, you'll be confident that you can deal with it.

The point is to practice using these tools, see what impact each exercise has, and find what works best for you. If you've applied all of these tools and done everything we've suggested, and you're still stuck in a negative mindset, it might be time to talk with a psychologist or personal coach.

Conclusion

We've introduced three life-changing and performance-changing skills in Stage II. Within each skill are numerous exercises and strategies you can use for an immediate impact. Whether in life or in preparation for a performance, these tools and skills will help you perform with confidence and boldness, free of the interference of overactivation, monkey chatter, and negative self-talk. This will help you create an optimal performance mindset so you can bring your mental best to your performance.

Think of the phrase "Ready, set, go!" Stage II is all about getting *ready*. It's all about physical and mental preparation. There is one final thing you need to do before your performance, though, and that is to declare your preparation complete. There are a lot of people who would laugh at this statement. They might ask, "How could my preparation be complete when there is always more I can do?" The declaration "My preparation is complete!" does not mean your preparation is *perfect*. It simply means you have done all you can and the time for improvement, adjustment, or practice is over.

This statement allows the brain to shift gears from practice mode into performance mode. In practice mode, there is an intense level of observation and comparison as you learn the skills. In performance mode, observation and comparison are shut off. A willingness to go with the flow and give your best is the new goal. Performers at all levels, in every domain in which we've worked and trained, have enjoyed the simple yet powerful statement "My preparation is complete!"

Now, it's time to put what you've practiced to the test. It's time to give your best. This declaration will help you focus on the actual execution during the performance.

With the declaration that your preparation is complete, you can close the door on Stage II and open the door to Stage III.

STAGE II: READY
(PHYSICAL AND MENTAL PREPARATION)
SUMMARY AND ACTION ITEMS

There are three key skills to help you prepare both physically and mentally for any performance: Skill #1: Activation Management; Skill #2: Positive Self-Talk; and Skill #3 Mindset Management

1. ACTIVATION MANAGEMENT

There are three areas of activation management to help you maintain an optimal level of activation. Use the exercises/activities that work best for you.

A. BREATHING EXERCISES

- Fist Squeeze (1–2 minutes)
- Fingertip (1–3 minutes)
- Paced Breathing (1–5 minutes)
- Fire and Ice (2–3 minutes)
- Progressive Muscle Relaxation (3–5 minutes)
- Fullness (2–5 minutes)

B. MINDFULNESS AND RELAXATION EXERCISES

- Sticky Notes
- Ring Tone
- Stoplight
- Walking Words
- Be Present
- Tapping

C. MEDITATION

- Find a style of meditation that works for you and practice it

2. POSITIVE SELF-TALK

This is about controlling the monkey chatter that exists in your mind and replacing it with what you really desire. Remember, "As a man thinketh, so is he!"

- Positive Self-Talk Strategy #1: Recognize the Monkey Chatter!
- Positive Self-Talk Strategy #2: Thinking Errors
- Positive Self-Talk Strategy #3: And
- Positive Self-Talk Strategy #4: Positive Affirmation

3. MINDSET MANAGEMENT

Designing an optimal performance mindset is a skill that requires practice. Many times, the most challenging part of mindset management is to stay in it, to hold on to it, and when it shifts, to remain calm. The key is to refocus and get right back into your optimal performance mindset.

CHAPTER 5
Stage III: Set (Pre-Performance Routines)

While on the bus traveling to a marching band competition, Mark, the drum major, had a thought that sent a wave of panic through his body: *I think I forgot to wash my gloves!* He quickly got out of his seat and grabbed his backpack, then frantically dug through it, praying the gloves were clean. He was activated! He just knew that if his gloves were dirty, he was going to drop the baton during the finale. He found the gloves, and, sure enough, the palms were a dingy gray from hours of practicing with his aluminum baton. His heart sank; his anxiety soared. He thought to himself, *How did I forget to wash my gloves? This is horrible!* It might not seem like a big deal to most, but to Mark, this was huge.

Because clean gloves were such an important part of his ritual, he just couldn't get out of his head. In his mind's eye, he repeatedly saw himself dropping the baton during the finale. At the next rest stop, he tried to wash them in the sink, hoping that would do the trick. Mark's "clean gloves catch the baton; dirty gloves drop the baton" ritual was now a source of anxiety and mental interference. Somewhere along the line, Mark had attached having clean gloves to a successful performance. And, not surprisingly, he dropped the baton during the finale. Did he drop it because his gloves weren't clean? No. What you've already seen in previous chapters is that Mark could have had a totally different outcome given the right tools. This is when the ideas in Stage III become so important.

The goal of Stage III is to have a *ready body* and a *focused mind*. This is the "set" part of the process of "Ready, set, go!" It is critical you understand that Stage III is the time between "declaring your preparation complete" (the end of Stage II) and the start of your performance (Stage IV). It is in this gap (usually within the twenty-four hours before an event or performance), between the preparation and the performance that people are likely to psych themselves out, which is exactly what happened to Mark. Unfortunately, he didn't know about the Five Stages of Peak Performance. How much better would Mark's experience have been if he had an optimal performance mindset, the skills to understand and optimize his activation, the knowledge to recognize his monkey chatter, tools to visualize success, and a powerful set of pre-performance routines. The truth is that it wasn't Mark's fault; he was simply doing the best he could with the knowledge he had at the time. Fortunately, Mark discovered these tools after his baton-dropping experience, and they have totally changed his life.

This is a good time to pause and remember that Stage III applies to any type of performance, whether it's public speaking, a sporting event, taking a test, a performance on stage, etc. In some cases, Stage III may only last a few minutes, with just enough time to declare your preparation complete and perform. During the time between ending your preparation (Stage II) and the actual performance (Stage IV), it is critical you do the right things to get you mentally and physically set!

Stage III consists of three important skills:

    1. Pre-Performance Routines
    2. An Optimal Performance Mindset
    3. Visualization ("Chairflying")

Pre-Performance Routines

An effective pre-performance routine does two important things: First, it brings the body into an awareness of the skills that will be needed for the performance. Athletes warm up before the game to be physically ready for the demands they will put on their body. Second, the pre-performance routine brings the mind into focus. This is where routine helps the performer close the doors to all the other areas of their life so that there is a singular focus and a mental readiness for the task at hand. It's when you're standing backstage, in the locker room, or at the doorstep of your next adventure that you want to be excited, ready, and focused so you have a great experience. What you don't want is to visualize something negative, like dropping the baton during the finale because your gloves aren't clean.

Finding the right routine takes some experimentation. This is where your coach and your experience will help you develop a routine that allows you to be at your best, both physically and mentally. Here are a few ideas to ensure that your pre-performance routine is geared toward a great performance.

PRE-PERFORMANCE TIP: MAKE A CHECKLIST

We recommend you start with a list, or what we like to call a checklist. Well in advance of your performance or activity, list everything you need to have in hand, or in place, so that when it is time to start your performance, you don't have to worry about what might or might not have been done. Fighter pilots use checklists. When Rob was flying F-16s, he was so familiar with the checklists they became second nature at each stage of flight—takeoff, air refueling, descent, landing, etc. Yet, even though it was second nature, he would still reference the checklist to ensure that everything was in order. This resulted in total confidence and focus for Rob; there were no worries such as, "Did I remember to make sure the landing-gear pins were removed?"

There are two primary checklists to consider: physical and mental/emotional.

1. THE PHYSICAL CHECKLIST: What do you need to be physically and logistically ready?

This checklist includes anything that might apply to physical preparation. Examples might include what time will you arrive, how you are going to get to the performance, what you will wear, when you will clean those items, when you will get dressed, what you need to look your best, and what you will eat. There may be other, more technical things to think about; for example, is the mic ready? A "simple" mic check may not be so simple. Is your laptop charged, or will you need a power cord? An athlete might need new spikes for their shoes or a new pair of hitting gloves. A musician might need to adjust the piano bench or oil the valves on a trumpet. Whatever it is you need to support your performance, add that to your list.

Here's a sample physical checklist for someone getting ready to give an important talk or presentation:

- Laptop charged
- PowerPoint backed up on a thumb drive
- Backup laptop
- Clicker
- Participant handouts
- Pre-call with the person in charge of audiovisual to ensure they have a VGA cable and speakers
- Microphone
- Clothing:
  - ☐ Dress shoes
  - ☐ Tie
  - ☐ Suit coat
  - ☐ Belt
  - ☐ Black socks

2. THE MENTAL AND EMOTIONAL CHECKLIST: What do you need to be emotionally and mentally ready? A few examples of what you might include in this checklist would be:

- My preparation is declared complete.
- Which breathing or mindfulness exercises will you use? When will you use them?
- What positive-self-talk applies to this event or performance?

- When will you review your optimal performance mindset?
- When are you going to use visualization?
- Say to yourself "I got this!" as you start your performance.

Every aspect of this stage should generate a proper mental focus that supports one thing—a successful performance! Once you've diligently run through your checklists, you will feel a sense of peace and confidence knowing that all loose ends are tied up. Declaring your preparation complete will free your mind to focus on the task at hand and eliminate any potential distractions.

In developing your pre-performance routines, be careful to stay away from "rituals." It's important to realize that there's a difference between the pre-performance *routine* and a *ritual*. Rituals are based in superstition—giving something irrelevant the power to impact your performance. Mark, the young drum major, knows all about the disruptive power of his "clean gloves" ritual, as do those who try to invent something that will give them an edge.

A ritual has no true bearing on outcome. Rituals might include things like the clean-glove example, a piano performer who runs their hands under warm water for exactly fifteen minutes prior to a performance, or an athlete who has to hit their hand on a sign before every game, and so on. A routine is like a checklist and is focused on the preparation so that potentially distractive variables are eliminated. A routine is all about true preparation, whereas a ritual is something conjured by a person's mind. And remember, while you may have developed the perfect routine, you will always be performing in an imperfect environment; thus, flexibility is an essential element of a routine. The more rigid you are with a "routine," the more anxiety you will likely experience if something doesn't go exactly as planned.

In the Air Force, flexibility is the key to airpower. It's also key to a successful performance. For example, we know a young, aspiring Broadway star who was excited when she got a call back for a big show she was auditioning for. She was a strong student of the Five Stages of Peak Performance and had mastered all the tools. Using her pre-performance checklist, she arrived forty-five minutes early, ready to engage in a combination of visualization, breathing exercises, vocal warm-ups, and even a few jumping jacks. She would be prepared when audition time came. When she arrived, however, she learned they were ahead of schedule and she only had ten minutes until her audition. So much for her ideal pre-performance routine! She quickly adjusted her plan and determined how she could make the best use of the shortened time frame. She got focused, did a few vocal warm-ups, a few breathing exercises, and reviewed her positive trigger words. That's all she had time for. And when she was called on stage, she had an incredible audition. Although she had a pre-performance routine all planned out, she was able to adjust to an unplanned situation. This is a perfect example of what can happen when someone is armed with the tools from all five stages.

You've just read about the ideal pre-performance experience. Now, do a self-check and ask yourself if certain rituals have made their way into your routines. If you discover that they have, take immediate action to eliminate them. You don't want your success hinging on your version of a "lucky rabbit's foot."

In Stage III (within the twenty-four hours prior to your activity or performance), it's important to use your decider brain, especially when things don't go as planned. This isn't the time to freak out, get mad, or listen to monkey chatter. This is the time to decide, call it good enough, and move forward. Ultimately, when it is time to start, you start.

Think about the twenty-four hours prior to your next performance. In a perfect world, what kind of routine, schedule, or checklist would you hope to follow to ensure your physical and mental readiness?

With a strong pre-performance routine, you have established a powerful system to support a great performance. Now the challenge is keeping yourself in the right mindset and optimally activated so you are ready to perform. This is where an optimal performance mindset and mental toughness come into play.

The Optimal Performance Mindset

In Stage I, you identified your vision and your why as part of the foundation for your performance or experience. You should have a clear picture of where you want to focus your attention and what kind of mindset you want to bring to this experience. This is where your trigger words really make a difference. "Bold, confident and free—that's me." Now it's time to maintain an optimal performance mindset and stay mentally tough. If your mindset begins to shift or you encounter a distraction, be prepared to refocus quickly. As mentioned previously, this is the time to be psyched up and not psyched out.

Our experience has shown there are several issues performers consistently encounter and which they need to be ready for in the pre-performance time frame in Stage III. We call these the "big six." These six different issues have the potential to throw a person off during this critical time directly preceding the performance. Once you're aware of them, it's fairly easy to guard against them and stay focused on the task at hand. Think about the worst performance ever that you identified in exercise one of the assessment. What thoughts and emotions did you experience? As you think about that experience, did any of what we call the big six show up? And if they did, how did you handle it?

Let's walk through each one of these issues so you can be aware of them and ready to handle whatever may show up:

1. OVERACTIVATION/ANXIETY: As discussed in the previous chapter, anxiety can pull your attention away from your upcoming performance and redirect it toward the monkey chatter that feeds the anxiety. This is commonly referred to as stage fright. If a person is focused on their anxiety, that person's focus is off target. This is why we emphasize the practice of daily relaxation and meditation as part of Stage II. Breathing exercises will only benefit you to the degree you practice them. The more you master the exercises in Stage II, the easier it will be to manage your anxiety and activation levels.

When a person shifts their attention away from the anxiety (using the techniques learned in Stage II) and back into the optimal performance mindset, the anxiety usually begins to fade, and they can focus on having a great experience.

2. THE FEAR OF FAILURE: Almost every person we've ever met has experienced the fear of failure at some point. The fear of failure is another source of mental distraction and is often accompanied by a lot of anxiety, despair, and even depression. This emotion can trigger your history of failure or cause you to relive past feelings of shame and embarrassment. Fear is almost always based on irrational thought. It can take you out of the present and into a fantasy about something that could happen but is unlikely to happen. This is when the skills of positive self-talk and visualization become so important. Positive self-talk and visualization remind you that you can take the outcome, positive or negative, and progress as a person or performer.

Ralph Waldo Emerson wisely said, "Don't waste life in doubts and fears; spend yourself on the work before you, well assured that the right performance of this hour's duties will be the best preparation for the hours or ages that follow it."

3. THE HAPPENINGS OF LIFE: Issues such as family discord, school-related stress, poor health, and so on can be very distracting. The goal of Stage III is for you to move away from these types of distractions and step into your performance or activity. You don't want to bring the worries of a chemistry test to your performance. All the skills, exercises, and techniques you've learned from previous chapters will be needed to eliminate these outside distractions. Rarely will you be able to immediately resolve it to your satisfaction, and so it's best to drop it or let it go for now, as it will not serve you. This will require you to access your decider brain and reset the priority for right now on your performance.

One of the best ways to clear your mind is to quickly talk things out with a trusted friend. If that's not an option, you can start the tapping exercise from Stage II. While tapping, follow this script:

"Even though I am feeling_____, I can let that go for now. My priority right now is_____. I love and accept myself. I love and accept this situation, and I want to bring a positive attitude of (list your affirmations) to this performance. Right now, this performance is my priority."

4. FEELING UNPREPARED: Another common issue is the last-minute feeling of "I'm not prepared!" In reality, a poor performance based on poor preparation is the easiest thing to fix. You just practice and get it right the next time (assuming there is a next time). However, the assumption here is that you have put in the practice and that some unnecessary distraction has begun to plague you.

The most important part of Stage II was to declare your preparation complete. People love this powerful declaration because it mentally frees you to confidently step forward without wondering if you've practiced enough.

If you're experiencing any lingering feelings of doubt, it's time to do a breathing exercise (Stage II), repeat your positive trigger words, and remind yourself that your preparation is complete.

5. NOT GOOD ENOUGH: This is monkey chatter! Negative self-talk causes self-doubt, which leads to anxiety and insecurity. This mindset often leads to a focus on pleasing the audience or meeting someone else's expectations, which is almost always the wrong motivation. The "not good enough" thought process is a reminder of how quickly thoughts and emotions from the past can leap into the present and really mess things up. The powerful affirmation "I am more than enough to handle whatever shows up" is a great way to challenge that negative monkey chatter while you remind yourself that you are in Stage III, you're ready, and you're excited about Stage IV—the performance.

6. SURPRISES: This is when something unexpected shows up and interrupts your focus and pre-performance routines—you forget your hat, there's a last-minute change of plans, or your instru-

ment or equipment malfunctions. If there is a surprise, you simply "cope" the best you can. This is when you need to be the decider and practice the first law of improvisation: "Yes, _____ happened, and this is how I will roll with it!" Humor is a great way to handle surprises. Another skill in these difficult moments is to stop thinking about what it would be like without the surprise. Roll with what you've got.

Remember, we talked about coping with surprises during Stage II. Top performers will intentionally introduce "surprises" into their practice so they'll know how to cope with whatever shows up.

Any one of the big six can show up and derail a performance if you're not aware of them. Armed with this knowledge, you're ready to handle whatever comes your way just prior to your performance or experience. When you combine the skills from all three stages, you'll feel confident and ready for what you're about to do!

Visualization ("Chairflying")

In the fighter-pilot world, the best fighter pilots chairfly prior to their flights. What is chairflying? Well, imagine all that goes into planning a complex mission. Normal mission planning for a single flight can take up to twenty-four hours; it's a detailed and complex process. Once the planning is done, the pilots gather in a room and spend about ninety minutes meticulously briefing each other about the flight from beginning to end. After the brief, each pilot has about fifteen minutes before they head for their jet. During that fifteen-minute break, between the brief and the flight, the best pilots will take between five and seven minutes to chairfly the critical parts of the mission. In other words, they sit in a room, close their eyes, breathe, and visualize what the practice attack will be like. They envision what the cockpit smells like, how it feels, what they should be seeing, the noises they'll be hearing, the attack numbers, etc. The objective of chairflying is to engage all five senses and make it as real as possible while in the quiet of the room so that when you're in the actual experience, you've already "been there." A fighter pilot is ready for the actual attack because they have "experienced" that attack while chairflying. The odds of flying a successful mission rise dramatically when a pilot is calm and able to stay ahead of the game because of their chairflying

As an F-16 instructor, Rob would come back from a mission and ask each student pilot whether they had taken the time to chairfly before the flight. In almost every case, he already knew the answer before asking the question. It was obvious in a young pilot's performance whether they had or hadn't chairflown prior to the mission.

Likewise, prior to any performance, the best performers take a few minutes before they step onto the stage, onto the field, or into the boardroom to chairfly the important parts of the experience. It's the final act of preparation prior to the performance.

Visualization has been proven as an effective peak-performance tool by countless performers from all walks of life. Unfortunately, if we're not careful, visualization can go the other way—in a negative direction. A person can visualize tragedy as well as triumph. Your thoughts, words, attitude, and dreams, as well as your fears, concerns, and frustrations can become part of your visualization. It takes a lot of practice to keep it positive, optimistic, and realistic.

For example, imagine someone standing at the free-throw line in an arena full of people, with just three seconds left in the game. It's an intense situation. The game is tied, and the player has one shot to win the game. The cheering of the crowd has become a deafening roar, and the player can see the longing hope in their teammates' eyes; they're praying the shot goes in. The stakes are high, and this scenario could cause an overactivation-type situation. But imagine rewinding the clock just two hours prior and the difference it would make had this player taken a couple of minutes to chairfly a situation just like this—the deafening noise of the crowd, the clock with only three seconds remaining, etc.? The player would now be standing at the foul line with the game on the line, but it wouldn't be the first time they'd been there. The player who's taken the time to chairfly a scenario is much more likely to be calm, collected, and focused as they take that game-winning shot.

Visualization plays an important role in each of the Five Stages of Peak Performance. In Stage I, a performer's vision must be powerful enough to generate a commitment to action. In Stage II, with mental and physical preparation, visualization helps the performer develop the motor skills necessary for the desired outcome. In Stage III, visualization is part of the pre-performance routine that enables a performer to access the motor skills and mindset needed to bring the best to their performance. Stage IV is when vision meets reality. Stage V, post-performance, is when visualization helps you target the things that can be improved upon the next time around. Though visualization is woven through all five stages, it is during Stage III that visualization is most critical. It should be a key part of your pre-performance routine.

There isn't a right or wrong way to use visualization. With practice, you'll discover what gives you the best results. Some people visualize watching themselves perform as if they were a member of the audience. Others see themselves as the performer. Some like to visualize every detail of the entire performance, while others go more for the general feeling of it. Others just visualize bits and pieces. It all depends on your situation and what you are going to be doing. The most important thing is to focus on practicing positive visualization.

Now that you understand how powerful visualization is when it comes to a successful performance, let's talk about how to do it. Ready to learn how to chairfly? Let's go!

How to Visualize (Chairfly)

STEP #1: CHOOSE A BREATHING OR RELAXATION STRATEGY FROM STAGE II.

Pick your favorite exercise from Stage II, set aside a couple of minutes, and begin by focusing on breathing and relaxing. Visualization is all about using your imagination. While you're doing your breathing or relaxation exercises, consider the first three stages:

Stage I: Vision and Motivation. Why are you doing this? And what is the attitude you have designed to support the entire performance process? Identify the trigger words you have set for this performance. Ponder on each word for a few breaths. *Bold. Confident. Free.* What do your trigger words mean to you?

Stage II: Mental and Physical Preparation. Review all the different things that are in place to help you have a great performance. Review the hours of practice, the commitment, and the effort. Mentally declare your preparation complete.

Stage III: Pre-Performance Routine. You've run through the checklists, your attention and focus are on the task at hand, and your preparation is complete. Feel confident in knowing you are ready.

STEP #2: VISUALIZE YOURSELF PERFORMING AT YOUR BEST.

Engage as many of the senses as possible and visualize yourself in the performance. Mentally put yourself in the situation. What do you hear? What do you see as you look around? What do you smell?

Once you've mentally put yourself in the situation, visualize yourself performing to the best of your ability. Go through the key parts of the performance and take some time to see yourself doing it perfectly. You can even visualize the end of your performance. See yourself being grateful for the opportunity to perform and humbly learning from the entire process.

Visualize only the positive. Don't even start to think about potential negatives.

Let's look at an example of how this is done. Rob has his children chairfly before each of their games. In this case, let's see how his daughter would chairfly in preparation for her soccer game. Below is an example of the questions he asks his daughter and the answers she gives him:

What are you seeing in your mind's eye from the perspective of your forward position during the game? *The other players, a sunny sky, the parents on the sidelines, etc.*

What does it smell like out on the field? *Grass.*

What do you hear? *People cheering.*

What do you see as you run down the field? *Running down the side, I see a defender positioned in front of me.*

What will you do when you get to the defender? *I see myself going around her, and now I'm about twenty yards out and it's just me and the goalie.*

Where will you put the ball? *I see myself dribbling up another few yards and then giving it a hard kick to the upper left-hand corner of the goal.*

What do you hear and see when you score the goal? *The crowd is cheering, and my teammates are running down the field toward me.*

At some point during the game, she will likely find herself in a similar scenario to the one she's visualized while chairflying. The same principle applies to the fighter pilot, the basketball player at the free-throw line, or any other experience you can imagine.

What's awesome about chairflying (visualization) is that anyone can do it. Although it should be one of the final things you do prior to your activity or performance, it can be used at any time in preparation for the actual event. When you engage your senses, you're engaging other parts of the brain and it becomes a type of perfect practice.

Next time you have an event, activity, or performance, set aside five to ten minutes to chairfly and see yourself having a great experience!

Conclusion

At this point in the performance process, you have defined your vision/goals, determined your motivation, and designed a mindset that supports the entire process. Having prepared yourself mentally and physically, you've declared your preparation complete. You've been practicing your optimal performance mindset. You have even practiced coping with surprises. You have followed a well-practiced routine to get mentally and physically set, you've experienced chairflying, and now you're ready for the performance or activity you've been preparing for.

Take one final, centering breath, repeat your trigger words, and take the stage. It's time for Stage IV—the performance!

STAGE III: SET
(THE PRE-PERFORMANCE ROUTINES)
SUMMARY AND ACTION ITEMS

This stage is typically within 24 hours (or less) of your performance. It's the time between declaring your preparation complete and the time you start your performance.

There are three key skills to help you prepare both physically and mentally for any performance: Skill #1: Pre-Performance Routines; Skill #2: An Optimal Performance Mindset; and Skill #3: Visualization ("Chairflying").

1. PRE-PERFORMANCE ROUTINES: In developing your pre-performance routines, be careful to stay away from "rituals." It's important to realize that there's a difference between the pre-performance *routine* and a *ritual*. Rituals are based in superstition—giving something irrelevant the power to impact your performance. A routine is like a checklist and is focused on the preparation so that potentially distractive variables are eliminated. A routine is all about true preparation, whereas a ritual is something conjured by a person's mind.

To help you develop a high-performance routine, consider developing both a physical and mental/emotional checklist. A checklist will give you a sense of peace and focus knowing that you've prepared and ready.

2. AN OPTIMAL PERFORMANCE MINDSET: This is about staying focused on the task at hand and avoiding any distraction that can take you off-focus. There are typically six big distractors that can come up just prior to a performance. The most important way to combat these potential distractors is awareness...simply being aware of what the big six are:

- Overactivation/Anxiety
- The fear of failure
- The happenings of life
- Feeling unprepared
- Not good enough
- Surprises

3. VISUALIZATION (CHAIRFLYING): Prior to any performance, the best performers take a few minutes before they step onto the stage, onto the field, or into the boardroom to chairfly the important parts of the experience. It's the final act of preparation prior to the performance. The objective of visualization or "chairflying" is to engage all five senses and make it as real as possible while in the quiet of the room so that when you're in the actual experience, you've already "been there."

CHAPTER 6
Stage IV: The Performance

Jon was walking through a store one night, and as he rounded the corner, he ran into Robbie, a former student. It was an exciting reunion for them as Robbie, a big smile on his face, gave Jon an enthusiastic high five and said, "Dr. Skidmore, my band and I played Friday night, and we sandboxed it!" This was the first time Jon had heard the term "sandboxed," but he knew exactly what it meant—the band had a blast and were in the zone. After Jon and Robbie visited for a few minutes, they went their separate ways, but in that brief reunion, it was clear Robbie felt the elation that comes with a peak performance.

There's nothing quite as rewarding as experiencing a peak performance. Think about a time in your life when you played in your "sandbox," or had a great time doing something—when everything came together and you felt awesome during that performance. It's likely you still felt the energy and exhilaration of the moment days later.

One thing we often hear in our interactions with the people we teach is how short Stage IV is (the performance) compared to the amount of time spent preparing for it. You may wonder why this chapter is shorter than those preceding it. A lot of time and energy, sometimes even a lifetime of time and energy, goes into the preparation and development of your skill—but the actual performance is over before you know it.

The performance starts and then ends. You did what you did and didn't do what you didn't do. The outcome was the outcome. It may have been a peak performance, but maybe it wasn't.

All that preparation culminates in the few seconds it takes a gymnast to run, launch, and land their vault, or in the thirty minutes it takes to finish the test or make a speech. Or sometimes there are those performances within the performance. Take, for example, the football season. The season starts and ends, just like each game starts and ends. The Five Stages can work as well for a season as they do for an individual game.

We've emphasized again and again how it's all about the preparation of your mindset and skill set. You may have heard the old saying, "When the time to perform arrives, the time to prepare is past." The goal of this book is to get you to the point where you experience an enjoyable and memorable peak performance. While it's true that there isn't a lot to talk about in the actual performance, there are a few things you need to be aware of when it comes to Stage IV, or the performance.

Set Proper Expectations

Wouldn't it be great if you could experience a peak performance every time you performed? It would, but does it happen that way? No. Thomas Watson has said, "The man who does not take pride in his own performance performs nothing in which to take pride." Regardless of how a performance goes, take pride in the fact that you are in the arena! Realize you'll learn something from each performance. The only wasted performance is one in which we learn nothing. Jump in with the mindset that you will give it your best and then learn from whatever happens. When a child hears their mother or father say, "Just do your best," they often feel an unnecessary pressure, and what they really hear is, "We expect you to do it right, or perfect."

We believe that every performance can be your "best" performance. In other words, even with all the challenges of a live performance, you still prepare and perform the best you can in that moment. Sometimes our best is a disappointment to us, but it's still our best in that moment.

You shouldn't expect a peak performance every time. There are just too many variables. But that doesn't mean you can't consistently perform well and continue to raise the bar. In statistics, there is a powerful concept called "regression toward the mean." In other words, there is an average. There are times when your productivity or performance are higher, and times when they're lower, but it's important to look at the average. Does the NBA all-star expect to have a forty-five-point game every time? No. Do they feel like a failure and want to quit if they only make nine points in the next game? No. They know how to handle success and failure and how to come back to their average, somewhere in the middle. The objective for anyone who wants to adopt the high-performance mindset is to continue to raise that average over the course of weeks, months, years, or even a lifetime. It's like the musician who at age seventy-six said, "My best is still ahead of me, that's why I practice *every* day!"

Have a mindset where you learn something from every performance. With the right expectations, you set yourself up for success. No matter what happens during the performance, you will learn from it and get better.

Perfectionism and Avoidance

In the first three stages, we talked about the habits top performers have developed to help them deal with anxiety and perform at their best. When high performers have a vision and the determination to see that vision come to fruition, their daily actions align with that vision. Although vision and determination are key, one thing to be mindful of in setting your performance expectations is a perfectionist mentality. Don't expect a peak performance every time you perform or get in front of people. Perfectionists tend to experience great highs—and terrible lows. They may have grand success in one area of their life, while other areas suffer. These people can push themselves to the point of destruction while they try to reach that perfect performance or experience every time. In many cases, the perfectionist hopes for the great performance while fearing the bad performance.

We have all seen the destructive effects of maladaptive coping in response to lows or missed expectations. Since things don't always go the way we want them to in a performance, it's important to be aware of what happens when things aren't perfect so we can use that as a stepping stone instead of it being a stumbling block.

One of the coping techniques of the perfectionist mindset is avoidance, which can be very costly to any of us. When a person thinks, *I am not doing that again,* they create an artificial sense of safety. The reality is that it's just a form of avoidance. Avoidance erodes self-confidence and prevents progression. Anytime someone's anxiety spikes and they cope using avoidance, whatever they are confronting in that moment becomes bigger, more powerful, and potentially overwhelming. Virtually every performer has experienced performances that don't go as planned. As you well know, pursuing a vision or goal involves lots of ups and downs. If you're reading this book, you're serious about your success and searching for ways to level up. It's exciting to see someone accept a challenge and embrace all that comes with it—even knowing there will be downs. At some point, we've all experienced feeling like we're not enough, then having a course correction and achieving what we set out to do. That's what it's all about!

You will be much more successful if you apply the right preparatory tools, set proper performance expectations, and develop the ability to cope with unexpected challenges.

Don't get caught up in perfectionism. Not every performance will be a peak performance, and that's all right—you will learn and improve no matter what happens given the right expectations and mindset!

The High-Performance Mindset

In our Becoming Your Best seminars, one of the first things we share is that becoming your best is both a mindset and a skill set.

We'll ask people which they think is more important. Overwhelmingly, people answer *mindset*. And they're right!

When it comes to performing, there is the mastery of the actual skill, and then there is the mastery of mindset. For example, in basketball, there are those skills associated with the game, such as dribbling, shooting, etc. And then there is the mindset that goes with being in front of a crowd, performing under pressure, etc.

The color of a karate belt indicates mastery of a specific skill set. We are not trying to develop a system of colored belts to describe the mastery of the mental performance skills, but your mastery of the mental skills will level up when you practice everything you've learned in the previous three stages. In Stage II, you rated yourself on three key mental skills. Since that self-evaluation, you have learned numerous mental skills. Hopefully you've had a chance to practice those skills and create new habits, since they will have a direct impact on your actual performance.

Because those skills tie so directly into your performance, please take a moment and reevaluate yourself using the table below (1 being poor, 10 being great):

	1	2	3	4	5	6	7	8	9	10
1. Activation (Anxiety) Management										
2. Positive Self-Talk										
3. Mindset Management										

What's interesting is that your current rating in these mental skills is producing a certain level of performance in whatever arena you're in. In other words, where you are today is what's producing your current outcome in the performance. Imagine the possibilities as you continue to develop your mental skills and rate yourself higher on the scale.

The stories of the performers in this book are about people who had more than a sufficient level of mastery when it came to the skill set necessary for a great performance. What most of these performers lacked were the mental skills (mindset) to support the expression of their particular skill set. It can be frustrating to have mastered a skill only to have a weakness in your mental skills undermine the performance. Prior to learning the Five Stages, our performers didn't have enough mastery when it came to activation, attitude, and mindset management, as well as visualization and post-performance debriefing. Because they didn't have the right mental skills training, their performances suffered. What should be exciting for anyone reading this is knowing that you now have the mental-skills training to improve your performance.

It's exciting to see those who attend our Conquer Anxiety seminars feel a huge sense of relief as they shift away from thoughts of inadequacy, self-doubt, and failure to feeling bold, confident, and empowered. They learn that it is the mastery of the mental skills that starts them on the journey to developing a high-performer mindset. This is why we congratulate you for taking the time to read this book. You have the most important part of the improvement equation—you want to develop the high-performer mindset and skill set!

In the Zone

Take a moment and recall a peak performance experience in your life. While you think about that experience, let's look at a concept called "flow," otherwise known as "being in the zone." In his groundbreaking research, Mihaly Csikszentmihalyi describes flow as a space or a zone where you bring the sum total of your preparation, performance mindset, level of energy, and focus to a single moment. It's when everything comes together, and you experience a great performance. Csikszentmihalyi explains the relationship between the demand of a task in relation to skill set and mindset. If a task is too easy, boredom, apathy, or distraction become the mindset. If the task is too difficult, anxiety, fear, disappointment, and embarrassment dominate the mindset. The brain is truly a peak-performance tool because "the zone" is found somewhere between boredom and anxiety.

Below you'll see what is called the "Flow Diagram." What you're looking for on this diagram is the point between the demands of the task and the level of skill. This point is called "The Zone." Notice that the vertical line refers to the demands of the task, from low to high. The horizontal line measures the level of mastery. The hope is that the point where the demands of the task and your level of skill meet is in the zone because that's when you're likely to have a great experience. If your skill level is low and the demands of the task are high, you'll probably feel anxiety. If the demands of the task are low and the skill level is high, you'll probably feel bored. It is not about achieving an expert level before someone becomes a peak performer. What's important is recognizing that anytime a skill level meets the demands of the task, a person is much more likely to have a great performance.

The Flow Diagram

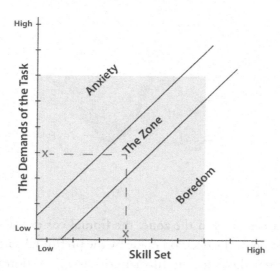

Think back to your peak performance experience. It's likely that the demands of the task matched your skill set and you were challenged enough that you weren't bored. Assuming you had the right mindset, you probably felt like you were in the zone.

Here are the characteristics of flow or being in the zone. As you look at them, see how well they describe what you experienced.

- There is a sense of ease.
- There are thoughts of neither victory nor defeat.
- You are in the moment, not the future or past.
- There is a feeling of enjoyment, excitement, and even exhilaration.
- There is a decreased sense of self-awareness.
- The demands of the task are being met.

The Brain in Flow

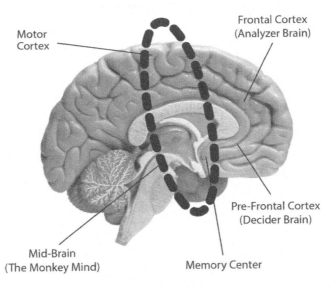

When a person is in the zone, the frontal cortex, or the brain's evaluator, accepts the decision made by the prefrontal cortex, which says, "You got this," and no further critical observation is needed. In addition, the midbrain, which controls fight or flight, perceives the confidence in "You got this" and that there is nothing indicating any threat or danger, so it remains deactivated. The motor cortex and the memory center, where the skills necessary to perform the task are stored, are uninhibited by the other parts of the brain and we have flow—until we don't.

A poignant example of this is when, in the 2006 Winter Olympics, US snowboarder Lindsey Jacobellis was racing down the snowboard course. She was in the lead and felt the exhilaration of being in the zone. Everything was in sync, and she was having one of the best performances of her life. Then, just one hundred meters from the finish line, she shifted her attention away from what she was doing and started thinking about the coming victory. When her thoughts shifted, it took her out of her flow, and during the final jump before the finish line, she attempted a celebratory "victory trick." To everyone's surprise and dismay, the snowboard slid out from beneath her and she skidded across the snowy course. The snowboarder who was in second place jumped into the lead and won the gold medal. Fortunately, Lindsey was able to get up and slide across the finish line in time to win the silver. And while a silver medal is great, she all but had the gold medal secured until she lost focus and slipped out of the zone.

Being in the zone is a combination of both mental and physical preparation, a combination of mindset and skill set. During the performance, it takes mental toughness and focus to stay in the zone.

It would be nice if you could perform at your peak every time, but as mentioned, that's an unrealistic and unfair expectation. With experience and practice, you'll strengthen your ability to mentally stay on task and be prepared for any surprises, breakdowns, or mishaps. And when, or if, these things happen, you'll experience an increased ability to cope—another hallmark of a high performer. The objective is to increase the frequency of those truly great performances and to raise the quality of the average performance. When that happens, those "poor performances" will lessen in frequency until they virtually disappear. For example, a concert pianist wasn't always a concert pianist. The concert pianist likely started when they were young and had both good and bad performances. Over the course of years and decades, the "poor" performances pretty much disappear. While the seasoned concert pianist may recognize an occasional mistake and admit it wasn't their best performance, to everyone listening, it was flawless and amazing. That's what we mean by continuing to raise the average. Eventually, your average will be amazing!

Conclusion

Imagine what it would be like in your next performance to have a blast and not have to think about it but instead just be in it. That's being in the zone. The lessons and skills you've learned about in the previous three stages are designed to give you the power to understand, minimize, and conquer anxiety so that you can optimize your performance and be in the zone on a consistent basis.

As you've advanced through Stages I, II, and III, you've discovered a new level of readiness to step out on the stage, the court, the field, or whatever your arena is.

Let's review all the things you've done up to this point so that you can have a great performance:

- You understand brain basics and the specific programming you've developed throughout your life. This programming is why you do and feel certain things.
- You developed a vision, goal(s), and identified what's driving you to do whatever it is you want to do.
- You've identified positive trigger words that bring you back to your vision and motivation.
- You've learned several powerful breathing exercises that will help you mentally and emotionally prepare for your performance.
- You've discovered how to use tapping and other calming techniques to settle your mind whenever it is overactivated.
- You understand monkey chatter and recognize the difference between it and reality. You now have positive affirmations you can use to challenge the monkey chatter.
- You've practiced in both the perfect setting as well as introduced chaos or unexpected events into your practice so that you're ready for the unexpected.

- You've developed pre-performance routines so that you can be 100 percent focused on the task at hand.
- You've declared your preparation complete.
- You're aware of the big six (fear of failure, happenings of life, etc.)—the things that can throw you off just prior to the performance.
- You know how to chairfly and can visualize a great performance prior to walking out into the arena (the stage, field, court, podium, etc.).
- You've set the proper expectations for your performance, and you're ready to learn something no matter how the performance goes.
- You understand the importance of being in the zone and the high-performer mindset to stay focused and in the moment during the performance.

Can you see why you are so prepared compared to how most people approach a performance or handle anxiety? As you implement what you've learned in each of the Five Stages, you'll feel an increased sense of confidence in your ability to go out and have a great time.

Now, enjoy the performance. All your preparation was for this moment. Tackle your adventure, share your talent, have fun, and enjoy it!

STAGE IV: GO (THE PERFORMANCE)
SUMMARY AND ACTION ITEMS

When it comes to the actual performance, it seems to be over in a flash. Sometimes a "flash" could be the few seconds it takes a gymnast to run, launch, and land their vault. Sometimes a flash could be the thirty minutes it takes to finish the test or make a speech. Then, there are also performances within the performance. For example, the football season. The season starts and ends just like each game will start and end. The five stages can work as well for a season as they do for an individual game.

The entire goal of this book is to get you to the point of an enjoyable and memorable peak performance – as you've read several times, it's all about the preparation of your skillset and mindset.

In Stage IV, there are some key ideas that will help you approach your performance the right way:

1. SET PROPER EXPECTATIONS: Regardless of how a performance may go, take pride in the fact that you are in the arena! You'll learn from each performance…the only wasted performance is the one in which we learn nothing. Jump in with the mindset that you will give your best and learn from whatever happens.

A performer can't control all the variables during a performance, but that doesn't mean you can't consistently perform well and raise the bar. Everyone has a "performance average" and one of your objectives is to consistently raise your performance average.

2. PERFECTIONISM AND AVOIDANCE: Don't expect a peak performance every time you perform or get in front of people. It's an unrealistic expectation and sets the midbrain up for anxiety. For many perfectionists who "fail," avoidance is the default coping mechanism. Remember, not every performance will be a peak performance, and that's all right—you will learn and improve no matter what happens given the right expectations and mindset!

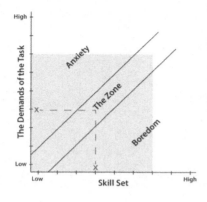

3. BEING IN THE ZONE: The point where the demands of the task and your level of skill meet is hopefully in the zone because that's when you're likely to have a great experience.

All your preparation was for this moment. Tackle your adventure, share your talent, and have fun!

CHAPTER 7
Stage V: The Post-Performance Debrief

A very frustrated student shared with Jon her confusion about a recent poor performance. She'd auditioned for the coveted first-chair violin position with the university orchestra and felt she was prepared, having run through each of the various stages so she could be totally ready. She'd expected to do well and had gone confidently into the audition. Yet, after the performance, she felt disappointed and frustrated. As she and Jon debriefed each stage, they soon found the problem. Stages I and II were solid—no concerns. The problem with her poor performance was found in Stage III. She had been number five in a line of eight violinists sitting outside the orchestra director's office. One at a time, they'd gone into his office to audition. As she listened to the auditions of the four violinists ahead of her, she'd started to doubt her own ability—the monkey chatter had begun. She'd wondered if she was good enough, she'd worried about what the director would think of her playing, and she'd started to compare herself to the other violinists. As you've probably guessed, she was activated, the monkeys in her brain were screaming. She'd forgotten all about the pre-performance routines she had planned to use and was consumed by her anxiety and doubt. To say she was off-balance when she walked into the audition would be an understatement.

She and Jon talked about what had broken down for her in Stage III and how it ultimately contributed to the difficulties she'd experienced during the performance (Stage IV). Then she made a list of things she would do differently the next time, such as setting the right expectations, using pre-performance routines to maintain an optimal performance mindset, challenging her monkey chatter, and even walking to another part of the building where she could be alone and visualize, or chairfly, a successful audition. Fortunately, she understood the importance of an effective post-performance debriefing and wanted to debrief the entire performance so she could learn from it. She was not afraid to look at what had happened and had the right attitude when it came to managing a disappointing performance. Courageous! Being able to accurately look at the entire performance experience and not just the missed expectation was invaluable. She was still disappointed in her performance, but at least the confusion was gone and she had a roadmap for how to improve the next time she performed.

The term we like to use for Stage V is called "debriefing." If you were to ask fighter pilots to describe in one word what makes them so good at what they do, the universal answer would be "debriefing." Pilots debrief after every flight. The average pilot debrief can last anywhere from one to six hours, and in that debrief, they'll do everything they can to remove ego from the equation. It's called a "nameless and rankless" debrief. The whole point is to find out *what's* right rather than *who's* right. We suggest approaching your performance debrief the same way: remove the ego and simply focus on getting better. While your debrief will likely be much shorter than a fighter pilot's, the goal is the same. It's to review lessons learned so you can repeat successes and eliminate setbacks and failures. This becomes a continuous improvement cycle as you raise your performance average.

Once you develop the habit of conducting a post-performance debrief, it shifts the way you view the performance. You're no longer attached to the perfect performance because you know that every time you debrief, you will find things that went well and things that can be improved upon.

So, what happens if a person skips Stage V and doesn't debrief after a performance? Let's take a look.

There was a very talented pianist who wanted help in overcoming her phobia of playing the works of Frédéric Chopin. In her early teens, she'd attempted to play a Chopin piece at her sister's wedding. It was a poor performance and she was deeply embarrassed. She even felt like she had ruined her sister's wedding. From that point forward, she'd refused to play anything written by Chopin. Even the thought of playing Chopin brought a wave of panic. Five years later, at the university level, her piano teacher insisted she include a Chopin piece in her senior recital. This requirement started a fresh, new wave of panic attacks.

Here again is an example of when a lack of performance skills, not ability, was the problem. Nobody had taught her about the post-performance debrief, and rather than learn from her early teenage setback, she was crippled by it. Five years later, she was doing everything in her power to avoid Chopin. Think about how this scenario could have been different if she'd understood Stage V and debriefed after the wedding experience. It still would have been embarrassing, but it would have been a learning opportunity rather than the source of a new fear.

Fortunately, it's never too late. After a five-year, belated debrief on the wedding reception, she finally realized what had caused her anxiety and poor performance. And rather than continue to avoid Chopin, she implemented the skills she learned from the Five Stages and noticed an immediate difference. A few months later, applying her newfound skills, she successfully performed her senior recital and had a wonderful experience in the process—even playing the Chopin piece. It was Stage V—the debrief—that finally freed this student to grow to love Chopin rather than fear him.

Throughout this book, we've talked about the power of the midbrain and the instinctive first response. Now you know that in the post-performance debrief (part of Stage V), listening to the midbrain, or monkey chatter, immediately following a performance isn't the best idea. Your first response shouldn't be trusted. The flash and flair of the first response is just that: flash and flair. The first response will be there whether you want it to be or not. The hope is that from this point forward, if you do have a negative first response, you acknowledge it but don't get stuck in it. If the only thing you get from this book is to label your first response as monkey chatter, then look for a second or third response, this book will have been well worth your investment.

If you recall Brad from the very first story in the book, you'll remember he was a master of post-performance bashing. He'd bludgeoned himself to the point of giving up his scholarship and his cello. Brad desperately needed the skill of debriefing. The best he could do with what he had at the time was a stubborn "I am not doing that again," and he stuck to it. For Brad or anyone else, it never has to be that way again!

How to Debrief?

Top performers in any field must master the post-performance debrief. As mentioned, the debrief starts with a clear understanding that every performance has something a person can learn from and improve upon.

There are three simple questions you'll answer in a debrief:

1. WHAT WORKED? There are always things that go well; you need to acknowledge these things and be grateful. In most cases, your list of all of the things that worked will be longer than the list of things that didn't. Some people mistakenly think that to debrief is to focus only on the things that went wrong. The reality is that you want to identify and acknowledge your successes so that you can repeat and build upon those successes.

2. WHAT DIDN'T WORK? Since a perfect performance is extremely rare, the idea is to look at failures or setbacks and ask what could be improved upon to prevent those failures and setbacks from happening again. Remember, even if you experience a major breakdown, it's not the end of the world. Your first response may tell you the world is ending, but when you look for a second or third

response, you can find a response that is a lot less dramatic and that contributes to your future as a performer. Although breakdowns can often feel embarrassing, you don't have to let a breakdown mean something negative. Learn to give breakdowns a meaning that moves you and your career forward. More often than not, how one copes with the breakdown is more important than the actual breakdown. The belief that a breakdown is the catalyst for a breakthrough is a belief you want to keep developing.

3. WHAT WILL I DO NEXT TIME? This starts on the premise that there *will* be a next time. This question creates forward movement as you explore how you can take what you have learned and use it to improve your next performance. It sounds so simple, and it is, but too often the flood of post-performance negative emotions is so powerful and overwhelming we can't even see what worked, let alone look for what will help us improve. Questions like "How would I handle it if a surprise like that happened again?" or "What is the meaning I want to give this performance?" or "How can I use this to improve next time?" fire up the frontal cortex, or analyzer brain. And with the shift from midbrain to analyzer or decider brain, you are dropping the drama of your first response. You are beginning to visualize the possibility of an improved performance rather than staying stuck in the black hole of disappointment.

Let's try an impromptu debrief. Think about a recent performance or experience that was important to you and answer the following three questions:

1. What worked?

2. What didn't work?

3. What will I do to improve next time?

In addition to asking these general questions about what worked and what didn't, you can get more specific by debriefing each of the Five Stages. The focus here is on the things you did or didn't do at each stage. For example, did you declare your preparation complete at the end of Stage II? This type of debrief broadens the performance and highlights the various factors that impacted that performance. It's like an elastic band: the elastic only maintains its flexibility when stretched. If the elastic isn't ever stretched, it will become stale and brittle. The point of going through each of the Five Stages during your debrief is to stretch you and help you learn from each aspect of your performance so that you don't become stale or complacent.

As you debrief each of the Five Stages, it's important to look at your attitude or mindset in each stage. In Stage I, you designed the mindset you wanted to maintain throughout the entire performance. So, by asking, "How did I manage my attitude in each of the Five Stages?" you start to recognize the impact a shift in mindset can have on your performance. How were you feeling in each of the stages? Were you confident, bold, and expressive, or were you frustrated, embarrassed, and negative? What caused a shift in your mindset? Every athletic team understands the impact of a shift in momentum. You must understand how a momentum shift impacts you and what you can do to slow the downward slide, then stop and make a U-turn.

Brad's Hypothetical Debrief

Let's see how Brad, the young cello player we met earlier, could have used a post-performance debrief. This is an example of the debrief Brad *could* have conducted but didn't—until years later. As you read this, remember that Brad didn't know about the Five Stages prior to his performance, so he didn't know how to manage his activation or how to do any of the things you've read about to prepare for his performance. Even though he didn't know anything about the Five Stages prior to his performance, this is how his teacher might have conducted the conversational debrief, going through each stage:

STAGE I: VISION AND MOTIVATION

Teacher: Brad, I'd like to debrief with you and run through what we call the Five Stages of Peak Performance so we can review your awards-assembly performance. Why did you decide to do this solo?

Brad: I was asked to perform at my high school awards assembly, where I was being recognized for the scholarship I received.

Teacher: How did you feel about performing?

Brad: I know I should have felt honored, but I felt like I had to do it for the orchestra director, and I didn't want to let him down. I didn't really want to perform in front of all of my friends.

Teacher: So, what was your attitude, or mindset, about actually performing at the awards assembly?

Brad: I really didn't want to do it. That was it. I didn't want to do it.

STAGE II: READY (MENTAL AND PHYSICAL PREPARATION)

Teacher: How did you prepare for this performance?

Brad: Well, it was really good in February when I practiced every day and auditioned for the scholarship. I hadn't played it much since then, but I thought that if I put in a couple hours of practice the day before, I would be fine.

Teacher: Did you follow your plan?

Brad: I practiced for about an hour the week before the performance and another thirty minutes the day of the performance. When I finished my practice before school, I was already getting nervous. I wasn't feeling very confident.

Teacher: Did you feel like you were ready?

Brad: Not really. There was so much more I needed to do. I just needed more time to practice. I thought I could get through it okay, but it didn't come back as fast as I thought it would.

STAGE III: SET (PRE-PERFORMANCE)

Teacher: What was it like on the day of the performance?

Brad: I got up early and practiced for about thirty minutes before school. I also had a chemistry test before the assembly. I was already nervous about the test, and then, when I thought of performing for the student body, I got really nervous.

Teacher: What did you do to try and manage your anxiety?

Brad: I just hoped I wouldn't mess it up too badly, and I pushed through it.

Teacher: Did you try and warm up and play it a bit before the performance?

Brad: I did, but all that did was make me more anxious. It was like I knew it was going to suck.

STAGE IV: GO (THE PERFORMANCE)

Teacher: Tell me about the performance.

Brad: When I walked on stage, I was shaking. It was so weird because I had never been that anxious before. My heart was pounding, and my hands were sweaty. When I sat down, one of my friends shouted my name, and that got me even more distracted. It's almost like my mind went blank. I tried to start, then forgot where I was, and I had to restart. It was so embarrassing. Because I had to restart, I was more nervous than I was before the assembly started. I made so many mistakes it didn't flow at all. I couldn't wait for it to be over. I couldn't believe how bad it was. As I walked off the stage, I thought to myself, I am done. I am never doing that again. It was too embarrassing.

Teacher: That sounds rough.

Brad: I don't ever want to perform again!

STAGE V: EVALUATE (THE DEBRIEF)

Teacher: Did anything about this performance work?

Brad: No!

Teacher: But you did it.

Brad: Well, I am not doing that again.

Teacher: Pause and breathe. You were really activated, weren't you? Did any part of it sound even a little okay?

Brad: Well, I got most of the middle section.

Teacher: So, there were a few things that worked . . .

Brad: Yeah, I guess there were some things that worked. I didn't think anything worked.

Teacher: If you were to perform again, what could you do next time that would help?

Brad: I would definitely need more than a couple of hours to get the song back into performance shape. I didn't need to get so freaked out by my friends in the audience, and I should have been more focused on the performance instead of being stressed by all the distractions. I sure am glad I didn't play like that for my scholarship audition.

As soon as Brad saw his performance through the lens of the Five Stages, he began to see more than his mistakes and embarrassment. The perspective that would have come from a debrief like this would have been so valuable. He likely would have realized that, although embarrassing, his poor performance wasn't the end of the world. In addition, he would have seen that there were so many things in his control that next time he would produce a totally different outcome. Because this type of debrief didn't happen in real life, he gave up on his scholarship. If he would have had a mentor or coach who understood the Five Stages and helped him debrief, he likely would have kept his scholarship and gone down a different path. This is the power of the debrief. It helps a person see through a clear lens and identify how to improve the next time around.

The Worst-Performance-Ever Assignment

One powerful debriefing tool is Jon's favorite assignment in his performance psychology class. He has each student write a description of their worst performance ever. Each student then spends three weeks examining their story, sentence by sentence, using the tools you have learned about in this book. These stories are generally dramatic and are often filled with disappointment, thinking errors, an all-or-nothing mentality, anxiety, grief, embarrassment, frustration, and even shame. The goal of this assignment is not to have the students dwell on the negative;

rather, it's to help them shift the lens from the negative and what they usually feel they can't control, to the positive and what they can control.

One day, three students in Jon's performance psychology class were asked to share their worst performance ever. As the third student finished his story, Jon recognized a common theme among all three performers. All had decided they would never again perform with that particular instrument because of their worst-performance-ever experience. That day, the trumpet teacher lost a student. The orchestra lost a viola player. The band lost a flutist. And the students lost whatever possibilities were available to them with those instruments. Unfortunately, at the time, these students lacked the skills to do anything but run. It is interesting to note that the kinds of experiences these students labeled their worst performances ever were typically seen as part of the process of learning their instrument and how to perform with it. You could even call these experiences developmental in nature, but the three musicians didn't see them through that lens.

They didn't know how to challenge their first responses, how to use the tools in each of the stages, or how to do a post-performance debrief. As a result, they were stuck in a cycle of post-performance bashing. Without the tools or debrief, they resorted to the same coping mechanism—avoidance. It worked, but at a high cost. Helping students turn their worst performance ever into a victory is always the goal of this assignment.

After three weeks of editing, rewriting, and practicing using these tools, the students develop a "victory statement." Below are five examples of actual worst-performance-ever stories rewritten as victory statements:

- "I learned that people can't determine my worth as a person based on my mistakes."
- "I am a finisher, not a quitter."
- "I discovered I can make mistakes and still finish boldly and confidently."

- "I discovered the importance of having a backup reed. I will never perform without one again."
- "Even with ample preparation, sometimes things happen that are out of my control. I can face adversity with composure and dignity."

Time to come up with your own victory statement!

If you go back to the assessment in chapter two, you already identified a worst performance ever in the fourth question of exercise one. Now, talk yourself through or write out your answers to the questions below. Doing so will help you to see your performance through the lens of each of the Five Stages. It will be even more effective if you talk it through or share your written answers with a trusted friend, teacher, or coach.

STAGE I: THE VISION

What was your performance goal or intention?

Why were you pursuing this goal?

What was your motivation?

What was your attitude, or mindset, like when you started the performance process?

STAGE II: READY

What did you do to prepare your skill set for this performance?

Did you have a sense that you prepared enough?

What was your attitude as you prepared for this performance?

Did you practice breathing and relaxation exercises on a daily basis to help with activation?

What self-talk did you use to challenge the monkey chatter?

Did you declare your preparation complete?

STAGE III: SET

What was it like just before the performance?

Did you do any visualization, or chairflying?

Did you have any pre-performance routines?

Were you able to block out the "big six" and focus solely on your performance?

What was your attitude during your pre-performance experience?

STAGE IV: GO

What were you expecting to happen?

What were your expectations for the performance?

What happened?

STAGE V: EVALUATE

What was your first response to this performance?

Did you do any kind of post-performance bashing?

Can you find anything good that came from that performance?

What did you take from that experience that you can improve on?

Pause, breathe, and ponder your responses to these questions. Can you find a victory in this performance? There is something of value there, so keep looking until you find it. If you just can't seem to find anything, it is time to share the story with a trusted friend or coach, because you are probably caught in a blind spot. And blind spots can be big!

From your post-performance debrief, write your victory statement (your big lesson learned) here:

Whatever you wrote down or thought about, the idea is that you can turn any experience or performance into a victory when you debrief and look at it through the right lens.

The post-performance debrief will help shift your mind away from the negative chatter to what you can control so that you can improve the next time around. Since a perfect performance is virtually nonexistent, there will always be successes to build on and failures or adjustments to learn from. Every performance or experience is a learning opportunity!

Post-Performance Bashing

In a recent conference, participants were asked, "How many of you consider yourselves experts in post-performance bashing?" About half the people in the room raised their hand. They were then asked to imagine what it would be like if they continued post-performance bashing after every performance, play, competition, game, talk, etc. It felt as if the air had been sucked out of the room. There were even a few audible groans.

Once people acknowledge how damaging negative self-bashing can be, nearly everyone wants to do something about it. There are three things every performer needs to know about post-performance bashing:

- First, it can be a strong habit based on past experiences processed by the midbrain. Post-performance bashing is a typical response for most.
- Second, a common belief is that being negative or beating one's self up post-performance will somehow improve the next performance. This is a false belief. The football coach who rips into the receiver for dropping the pass believes he is doing something that will help the player improve his performance. If the receiver catches the next pass, the coach feels like his tirade has paid off—it must have worked. If the receiver drops another ball, the coach

may think he needs to be even more harsh. There is no evidence to support the belief that yelling at a player improves their performance. Yet we often see performers of all types who make their situation worse by verbally and mentally beating themselves up after a performance. When a person figuratively yells at themselves, it doesn't improve their performance; to the contrary, it actually hurts future performances.

- Third, a post-performance debrief is so much more effective than post-performance bashing.

At the same conference where participants were asked what would happen if they continued to practice post-performance bashing, the question was then flipped. The audience was asked what it would be like if they practiced a post-performance debrief instead of bashing after every performance, game, project, talk, athletic event, or competition. It was as if a breath of fresh air had filled the room. There were smiles all around as the participants saw the possibility of a much more successful and enjoyable future.

From this point forward, we invite you to replace post-performance bashing with the post-performance debrief and make every performance a victory.

Story-Busting

In addition to developing lessons learned and replacing the post-performance bashing, there is another purpose to debriefing. When it comes to anxiety, it's helpful for people to rewrite their story. We call this story-busting. Story-busting is another powerful form of debriefing. We each have an internal story, or narrative, built on years of experience and programming. To understand and conquer anxiety, it is essential to rewrite your story. Whether it's a particular event or an issue from your everyday life, it's important to understand the story behind it, and, when necessary, go story-busting!

Below are six prompts that, when considered openly and honestly, will help you story-bust in relation to any performance or life experience:

1. Describe the incident.

2. Identify your thoughts about what happened.

3. Identify your feelings about what happened.

4. Describe your actions.

5. Where have you felt this before? Be willing to explore the depth of your feelings and go beyond the present situation.

6. What is the next right step?

As you answer these questions, look for a consistent theme. It's common to see negative themes emerge, such as "I'm not good enough" or "I'm worthless." It's time to take those negative themes or stories and bust them!

Story-busting starts with identifying the facts and clarifying the meaning you've given to those facts. As you look at the meaning, or story, you get to decide if that is the meaning you want to keep. Then you can determine if the meaning you attributed to that event has a cost attached to it or whether it creates a story that propels you forward. Each of us has stories from past events that are negatively influencing us today. This is one reason everyone can benefit from story-busting.

Sometimes the theory behind story-busting is difficult to understand, so let's get into the specifics of how to actually do it, and then you can try it with your own experiences.

There are five parts to a story:

PART I: THE FACTS   What happened?

PART 2: THE MEANING   What was the meaning you assigned the facts?

PART 3: THE COST   What will it cost you if you continue to believe the meaning you've given this experience?

PART 4: THE TWISTED PAYOFF   Feels like it can keep you safe and supports what you have believed about yourself up until now.

PART 5: THE POSSIBILITY   Find a new meaning that moves you forward. To step into a new possibility, you need to drop the twisted payoff, stop accepting the cost, and choose to take action.

The diagram below outlines this process. It begins with an event; this could be any performance or life experience. With any event, there is an automatic first response. We often go from event to response so fast that we miss the story or our history that is behind our response. The first response itself is not the problem; it's getting stuck in the first response that is the problem. The story-busting process will get a person out of the mud and moving forward.

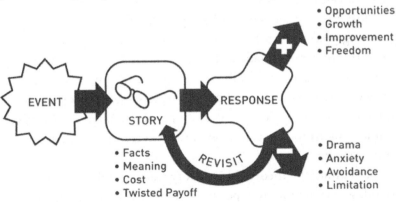

Earlier in this book, we shared the story of the girl at the climbing gym who was stuck in her story. She incorrectly thought that the 5.2 on the wall was a height requirement. Since she was just under five feet tall, she mistakenly thought she was too short to climb at that gym. Let's use this story to illustrate how each step of the story-busting process works.

PART 1: THE FACTS

She was part of a class activity at a climbing gym.

There was no mention of any participation restrictions based on height.

She had been properly trained to climb and rappel along with all of the other students.

She was wearing a climbing harness.

There were lots of numbers (difficulty ratings), ranging from 5.5 to 5.11, on every climbing route in the gym.

There was a 5.2 (which was actually a 5.5 with a scuff mark making it look like a 5.2) on the wall.

She was standing there, not engaged in the climbing experience.

PART 2: THE MEANING

She thought the 5.2 point was a height requirement and that since she was less than five feet tall, she was prohibited from climbing.

PART 3: THE COST

Participation in the activity.

The discovery of a new hobby.

The fun and excitement of climbing and trying something new.

PART 4: THE TWISTED PAYOFF

She didn't have to try anything new or leave her comfort zone.

She found even more evidence that her height was an acceptable limiting factor for her.

PART 5: THE POSSIBILITY

>The 5.2 was a difficulty rating, not a height requirement.
>She was free to climb and experience something new.
>She had been sufficiently trained to participate, and there
>   was nothing to hold her back.

What was the result for this young lady? Instead of sitting on the sidelines, she was able to climb and had an incredible experience. She had busted her story!

When you completed the assessment in chapter two, you accessed your memory bank of stories to fill in the blanks. Consider that each s on the sentence-completion questionnaire is just a one-line story and you have already labeled it as negative or positive. Part of conquering anxiety is being willing to find the stories from your past that negatively impact you today. In that spirit, pause for a couple of minutes and read through your answers in chapter two. As you read your answers, look for stories that may currently be creating limitations or stress in your life.

Pause here and read through your answers in chapter two.

Assuming you just went through chapter two, let's practice story-busting with one of your experiences. Choose one of the one-line stories in your assessment you would like to work on right now.

Write the chosen event, or one-line story, on the line below and then go through each of the story-busting steps:

_____

PART I—THE FACTS What are the facts?

PART 2—THE MEANING What was the meaning you assigned the facts?

PART 3—THE COST   What will it cost you if you keep believing the meaning you've given this experience?

PART 4—THE TWISTED PAYOFF   How does this story keep you safe? How does it potentially keep you stuck in old, limiting beliefs?

PART 5—THE POSSIBILITY   Find a new meaning that moves you forward. To step into a new possibility, drop the twisted payoff, stop accepting the cost, and choose to take action.

Story-busting is a powerful way to edit your old stories and mental programming. The facts won't change, but the meaning associated with those facts will. And with new meaning comes new possibilities and choices.

Just an awareness of story-busting alone is enough to transform many of the stories that have previously impacted our lives in a negative way. In other situations, awareness of the story is the starting point—like opening the door to the climbing gym with the intention to learn how to climb. It is also important to recognize and accept that some stories are so big and seem so true, that it might require the help of a coach or professional to help you work through that story.

It's important to know that grieving will sometimes be a big part of your story. It's all right to grieve as that can be a natural part of the process when dealing with a loss. Exploring grief and how to effectively grieve is beyond the focus of this book, however, we believe that effective grieving is on par with visualization – it is a peak performance skill. It's important that you remember that story-busting can bring out a wide array of emotions, but that is often a part of the process. Just realize that if certain emotions, such as grief, surface while doing this exercise, that's okay! If you get stuck or overwhelmed and can't seem to break free, it's most likely a big issue. With big issues, talking it through with a psychologist, coach or trusted friend can help.

Once you identify the negative themes running through your stories, you can incorporate some of the strategies and exercises from previous chapters to change those stories. For example, this is a great opportunity to conduct a tapping exercise, where you correct thinking errors or use a release-and-replace statement. Every time you work through a negative thought or experience, you build new neural pathways in your brain. The neural pathways associated with core beliefs are old and ingrained. If you're story-busting for the first time and you're focused on a big life experience, it can often take more than a few attempts to break through and create new neural pathways.

Story-busting opens the door to why we believe and act in certain ways. It's precisely why story-busting is included in Stage V—it's a powerful way to evaluate and debrief the experiences that have happened throughout our lives. Once we're aware of the underlying meaning we've attached to an experience, we can go to work changing that meaning and the impact that story has on our life!

What Now?

We've talked about how to debrief, how to avoid post-performance bashing, and how to rewrite our stories regarding previous experiences. So, what about when you finish your performance? What can you do right now?

Here are a few things from earlier in the book you can use during the post-performance experience to help you move forward with the right mindset, regardless of how the performance or experience went.

1. The next time you get worked up, stressed out, or want to run from a bad performance, pause and breathe. Listen to the monkey chatter, call it monkey chatter, review the debrief questions from earlier in this chapter, and see what happens to all that drama caused by the monkey chatter. Practice turning distorted thoughts into supportive thoughts.

2. Sometimes the chatter can be so strong and convincing you'll need to talk it through with a trusted friend or coach. Often, talking with another person helps us realize how distorted our own thinking is.

3. Read through your vision statement and goals, then review the situation you are struggling with in the context of your vision. Use the questions from Stage I to come back to your why. What are you doing? Why are you doing this? What mindset have you designed to support this performance?

4. Doing one of the breathing or mindfulness exercises from Stage II will help you become present, aware, and calm. The ability to breathe and relax is now a powerful tool in your quiver of techniques.

5. Think about and verbalize the positive affirmations you've come up with and consciously replace the monkey chatter with these affirmations. This may not be easy for the first one or two minutes but stick with it. Positive thinking is an integral part of shifting your mindset. It reduces the level of stress hormones and improves physical health. A great time to think about and recite your affirmations is while doing your breathing exercises. Remember, you're literally creating new neural pathways while reciting your affirmations.

6. Use a release-and-replace statement (just another form of affirmation). One way to do this is to release the negative thought and use your affirmations to affirm the positive.

For example, *I used to believe the audience was the enemy. Now I believe the audience is full of people I can share my message with.*

Here are some other release-and-replace statements:

I acknowledge the error in _____, and I replace it with_____.

I forgive myself for believing_____, and now I affirm_____.

_____ is false, and _____ is the truth.

Up until now, I _____, and now I _____.

There are certain situations, such as in a performance or an emotionally charged life event, where meditation, breathing exercises, and tapping can effectively help you deactivate and calm your mind and body. While it is almost impossible to let something go or even see it clearly when you are still in your first response, whether that be anger, frustration, or disappointment, a breathing or tapping exercise can help you calm down and break out of that anger or frustration. Sometimes the mantra "Sit down, shut your mouth, and breathe" can be a relationship saver, if not a lifesaver; it stops you from creating even more wreckage from any prolonged tirades. Once you are calm, the important work of debriefing and processing your emotions can begin.

Here are a few things to consider when meditating or breathing: Yes, it happened, and I responded with_____ (your response), but what is behind my response? Where is this coming from? When have I felt this before? What else does it remind me of? Where in my past have I felt this same thing? What was the belief that turned this present-day event into a drama?

It is likely that at the root of your feelings is a familiar attitude or core belief. As mentioned previously, look for themes of "I'm not good enough" (or worthless, bad, wrong, stupid, a disappointment). We tend to have a lot of energy around familiar beliefs. Stage V and these questions are a great place to see where history repeats itself.

These are just a few of the tools from this book you can use after a performance or an emotional experience. Each one is powerful in its own way, but when you combine all of them, you create a chemistry of excellence!

Conclusion

Each of the ideas in Stage V is designed to help you move forward rather than getting stuck in a particular performance or life event.

As we wrap things up, let's do an exercise that brings the entire chapter together.

> STEP 1: Go to AnxietyConquer.com to get a printable debrief sheet. Make five copies or print out five sheets of the debriefing page.

> STEP 2: Identify five poor performances or challenging life experiences and then, using the debrief template, do a debrief for each of those experiences.

> STEP 3: When you've finished all five debriefs, reread them and look for common themes. Can you see what triggered your midbrain? Completing these five debriefing pages will put the spotlight on the beliefs behind why you are experiencing the emotions you're experiencing.

Think about how different your approach to challenging performances or circumstances will be compared to how most people deal with similar situations. Hopefully, as you recognize post-performance bashing and first-response monkey chatter, you can apply specific tools to get your mind in the right spot and then do a thorough debrief to repeat successes and improve on setbacks or failures.

Every performance or experience is an opportunity to learn, grow, and improve. The focus on the post-performance debrief is about taking whatever lessons you've learned and applying those to the future in this journey of becoming your best.

STAGE V: EVALUATE (THE POST-PERFORMANCE DEBRIEF)
SUMMARY AND ACTION ITEMS

The goal of this chapter is to help you learn how to debrief important performances or experiences in your life. The debrief will help you review lessons learned so you can repeat successes and eliminate setbacks and failures. This becomes a continuous improvement cycle as you raise your performance average.

Once you develop the habit of conducting a post-performance debrief, it shifts the way you view the performance. You're no longer attached to the perfect performance because you know that every time you debrief, you will find things that went well and things that can be improved upon.

There are a few key ideas to help you effectively evaluate and improve:

1. HOW TO DEBRIEF? There are three key questions to ask yourself after each performance or experience:

    A. What worked?
    B. What didn't work?
    C. What will I do next time?

2. THE WORST PERFORMANCE EVER ASSIGNMENT: The goal of this assignment is not to dwell on the negative; rather, it's to shift the lens from the negative and what people usually feel they can't control, to the positive and what they can control. Take your worst performance ever examples from your assessment in chapter two and, with that experience in mind, debrief each of the questions from the Five Stages of Peak Performance (found in this chapter).

3. POST-PERFORMANCE BASHING: Many people consider themselves experts in the post-performance bashing. From this point forward, we invite you to replace the post-performance bashing with the post-performance debrief and make every performance a victory.

4. STORY-BUSTING: In addition to developing lessons learned and replacing the post-performance bashing, there is another purpose to debriefing. When it comes to anxiety, it's helpful for people to rewrite their story. We call this story-busting. There are five parts to a story:

> PART 1: THE FACTS   What happened?
>
> PART 2: THE MEANING   What was the meaning you assigned the facts?
>
> PART 3: THE COST   What will it cost you if you continue to believe the meaning you've given this experience?
>
> PART 4: THE TWISTED PAYOFF   Feels like it can keep you safe and supports what you have believed about yourself up until now.
>
> PART 5: THE POSSIBILITY   Find a new meaning that moves you forward. To step into a new possibility, you need to drop the twisted payoff, stop accepting the cost, and choose to take action.

While it may seem simple, story-busting is a powerful way to edit your old stories and mental programming. The facts won't change, but the meaning associated with those facts will. And with new meaning comes new possibilities and choices.

CHAPTER 8
Conclusion

Sheri sat there, head down, trying to hold back the tears and reeling from embarrassment and confusion. Everything had been going great—until it all blew up. She replayed the performance in her mind and couldn't figure out what had gone wrong. For some unknown reason, her accompanist had stopped playing in the middle of Sheri's solo. They'd prepared well and felt ready and had never had this problem before. There, in the middle of their performance, things had fallen apart and they'd looked at each other in panic, huge waves of embarrassment crashing over both of them. This was not supposed to happen. This was bad! They didn't know what to do, so they simply walked off the stage and tried not to cry. Unfortunately, Sheri was so embarrassed that, in the heat of the moment, she made a life-altering decision. She decided to end her singing career—at the young age of fourteen.

Sheri felt like she made the right decision; she didn't want to ever have another embarrassing experience like that. But when you read her story knowing what you now know about the brain and the Five Stages of Peak Performance, you can probably see several things Sheri could have done instead of giving up. Like so many of the performers we've discussed in this book, Sheri had the talent; she simply lacked the mental-skills training to manage a difficult experience. And without those skills, she didn't know how to move forward. In her mind, the only viable option was to quit so that she wouldn't ever have to worry about something like that happening again.

Like Sheri, we would all like to experience a peak performance every time we perform. It would be fantastic if that's how it worked, but is that how it really goes? No. There are too many variables in life, especially during a live performance, and a person can't presume to control all of these variables and be at their best every single day. That's an unrealistic expectation for anyone.

One of the key contributions of *Conquer Anxiety* and the Five Stages is to shift the context of a performance away from outcomes such as good or bad, win or lose, success or failure and instead foster a growth mindset. Sheri knew nothing about the Five Stages, and so her focus was on what she perceived as the outcome—*failure*. She was so embarrassed by her *perceived* failure that her decision-making about the future became an all-or-nothing proposition. Whenever someone is focused on the outcome, it's likely to trigger lots of monkey chatter, distraction, and anxiety.

Instead of focusing on the outcome, we need to learn to see every experience or performance as part of the process of becoming better. This is what the Five Stages are all about. Nobody starts at the top. It's a process that involves lots of grit and lots of practice. Becoming your best is a natural progression of growth, development, and maturity all tied into one word: experience. When someone is learning a new skill, it's easy to expect too much too soon, and that expectation has the potential to cause disappointment and feelings of failure. But the experience gained through repetition, practice, great performances, poor performances, and so on is invaluable.

So, rather than focus on the outcome, *we invite you to focus on learning from each performance in the process of gaining experience.*

What's great about the Five Stages is that they help you to learn and have the right experiences at a faster rate!

High-Performance Factors

Becoming a top performer in any arena of life means being willing to look at all the factors that influence your performance.

Consider four factors that influence any experience or performance:

- Your skillset
- Your mindset and emotional health
- Your body and physical health
- The environment where you are performing

The tools and ideas within the Five Stages can influence each of these areas. Within these areas, there are things you can control and influence and things you cannot control (which you'll need to adapt to). It's wonderful when the four areas all come together in a peak performance.

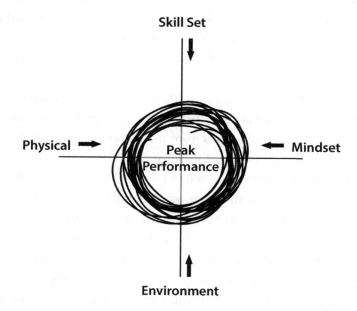

Will these four areas always perfectly overlap? Probably not.

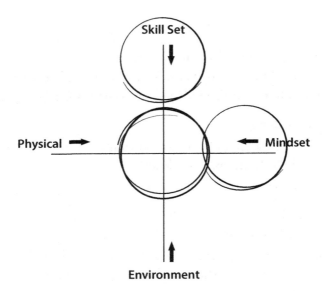

Environment

But when you apply the Five Stages, you are doing everything you can to bring them as close together as possible for that performance. The next time you perform, there are going to be variables that are closer to the center (the peak performance) and others that are more distant. If yesterday you were feeling great, but today your pet died and you are upset, you could naturally anticipate that your mindset will be further away from the peak-performance center. And the further the mindset is from the center, the more likely it is to negatively impact your performance.

For many, anxiety can become so overwhelming it physically debilitates them, in turn throwing off their mindset. Now that you have learned about your stress response, as well as activation and deactivation, you can move forward and through moments of anxiety. Isn't it wonderful to know you're armed with the skills you need to bring yourself closer to the peak-performance center? It's exciting to see how the mastery of the skills and tools in this book work together to bring these four areas into better balance.

Let's look more closely at these four areas and how they apply to your specific situation.

Skill Set	Physical Health	Mindset	Environment
• Your past performance experiences • What you have mastered for this performance • Specific things needed for this performance • Your warm-up to bring everything into focus	• Your level of positive energy • Your level of stress, anxiety, or activation • Your quality of sleep • General health • Nutrition • Level of physical conditioning and stamina • Meditation and rest	• Default mindset and monkey chatter • Designed mindset • Vision • Positive self-talk • Flow • Positive attitudes toward practicing • Coping with surprises/setbacks and breakdowns • Your overall mental health • Past performance traumas	• Weather • Temperature • Lighting • Others performing with you • Technology • Traffic • Something out of place

Environment can be tricky. There are things you can and can't control. For example, if the microphone stand is too low, you can raise it. If something is in the wrong place, you can move it. But when some sort of environmental "surprise" crops up, it is best to drop the expectation of what you thought things would be like and fully accept the way things are and then try to make the best of it.

Accepting the challenge and the reality that you are trying something difficult is exciting when you are willing to embrace the process and accept all that comes with it.

If you do a quick mental review of each of the Five Stages of Peak Performance, you'll see that they put you in a position to enjoy life and perform at your best. The Five Stages will impact your mindset, physical health, skillset, and even help you control many of the variables in your environment. That's why it's important to not just read this book once but, rather, treat it as a manual or guide. You'll want to come back to it again and again to identify additional areas of growth while you continue to raise your performance average and improve your ability to conquer your anxiety.

Our Promise

We've watched thousands embrace the Five Stages of Peak Performance and have found that there are three things that happen consistently. First, the willingness to perform increases. Second, the quality of the performance improves, resulting in a new and higher performance average. In other words, there are more frequent great performances and fewer "terrible" performances. Third, we see an increase in the enjoyment, fun, and excitement within the various dimensions of the performance process. We promise that when you apply the tools from each of the Five Stages, they will transform your life. It will take effort and practice, but the reward is worth it.

Although you'll benefit from using the ideas in just one or two of the stages, these tools will have the biggest impact if you implement all Five Stages. Below, you'll find a summary of the Five Stages. We invite you to mark the corner of this page so that you can refer to it again and again.

As you review this summary, think about an important upcoming experience or performance.

THE FIVE STAGES OF PEAK PERFORMANCE

STAGE I: VISION AND MOTIVATION

- What is your vision?
- What goal will help you work toward achieving your vision?
- Why are you pursuing this goal? What is your motivation?
- How are you committed to being as you pursue this goal?

Write the three trigger words that describe how you are committed to being as you perform.

Trigger words:

_____   _____   _____

STAGE II: READY!

- Skillset acquisition and mastery—practice, practice, practice!
- Which breathing exercises have you used?
- Which mindfulness and relaxation exercises have you used?
- Have you been meditating and chairflying?
- What positive affirmations are you using to challenge the monkey chatter?
- What thinking errors have you identified in your life?
- How are you being as you prepare to perform?

Important: Declare your preparation complete! Declaring your preparation complete allows you to perform with freedom.

STAGE III: SET!

- Get yourself mentally and physically set to perform.
- Go through your physical preparation checklist, which includes things like your uniform, your props, your transportation, your food, your instruments, etc.
- Go through your mental and emotional preparation checklist, which includes positive self-talk, activation management, visualization, etc.
- Are you distracted by any of the Big Six as you get ready to perform? If so, acknowledge that and refocus.
- Review your pre-performance, or warm-up, routines. No Rituals!
- Review your trigger words to access your optimal performance mindset.
- Are you feeling confident, expressive, and bold?

STAGE IV: GO!

- Set proper expectations. Each performance is an opportunity to learn. Perfection is not the expectation.
- Step into the sandbox; stay in the sandbox. Go play and have fun!

- Stay in the moment and go with the flow. Be in the zone.
- No thoughts of victory; no thoughts of defeat! Simply focus on the moment and enjoy the experience, no matter what happens.

STAGE V: EVALUATE

- No post-performance bashing! Each performance is an opportunity to grow your experience.
- Some things will work, and some things won't; plan to debrief after each experience.
- What worked?
- What didn't work?
- What will you do next time?
- Do you need to do any type of story busting to reframe your experiences?
- Learn from each experience and move on to the next so that you can increase your performance average.

What's Next?

As we head toward the homestretch, the focus becomes you. In other words, what will happen in your life going forward?

Here are five tips that will help you maintain focus and momentum:

MOMENTUM TIP #1: VISUALIZE

Pause and do your favorite breathing exercise or meditation until you are relaxed. If you're not already doing it, it's powerful to do at least one breathing exercise per day. Once you are relaxed, ponder the questions below. An effective pondering strategy is to focus on your breathing. When you inhale, ask yourself the question, and when you exhale, simply be still. Do that three to five times before you allow your mind to think about the questions again. Just be with the question and relax; there are no right or wrong answers. In addition to reading this, you can also go to

www.AnxietyConquer.com and do the "Three Promises" visualization exercise.

Here we go:

1. What kind of impact would an increased willingness
    to share your talents have on your life? What needs to
    change so that you are more willing to put yourself out
    there? What would an increase in willingness to perform
    actually look like?
2. Imagine what an increase in the quality of your performing
    would look like? What do you need to do the take your skill
    set to the next level? What is the first step in taking your
    skill set to the next level? When are you going to do that?
3. Imagine what it would be like to see your level of enjoy-
    ment increase. What do you enjoy about what you are
    performing? What would it be like to more fully enjoy the
    entire performance process? See yourself enjoying what
    you are performing. Go to that experience and make the
    visualization as vivid as possible. Soak it all in!

MOMENTUM TIP #2

Identify one important performance or experience coming up
this week and apply the Five Stages. This could be doing something
at work, an athletic event, a big issue you've wanted to address, or
anything else that's important to you. It takes sixty to sixty-five repetitions to make something a habit; it's the application of the tools
in the Five Stages that will make a difference. In other words, this
isn't a book you *read*, it's a book you *live*. So, identify one important
experience or performance this week in which you could apply the
tools found within the Five Stages.

MOMENTUM TIP #3

Visit www.AnxietyConquer.com and follow the links to enroll in
the online course. It's a powerful way to take these ideas, concepts,

and exercises to a much deeper level in your life. It will give you the chance to practice many of these exercises combined so that you can see how we do it. Sometimes just watching another person do it helps bring it all together.

MOMENTUM TIP #4

Come back and reread Conquer Anxiety two to four months after applying the different tools and exercises to your life. It's amazing how many people say they get more from the book the second time around. This partly has to do with how the brain learns and retains information. You're likely to be in a much better place the second time you read it. It will be exciting to see how your answers in the assessment change over time.

MOMENTUM TIP #5

Follow us on social media for updates, new research, and important announcements at

- www.AnxietyConquer.com
- Facebook: Search for *ConquerAnxiety* and join the group to get free videos, courses, thoughts, and to share any of your ideas or perspectives.

These tips will help you maintain your momentum and continue moving in the right direction. Change is rarely easy, but it's worth it. Mastery of a skill or habit takes time, effort, and repetition. Since it takes sixty to sixty-five repetitions to create a habit, it rarely happens overnight. It also means that with determination and persistence, you can experience massive change in your life when you master the different tools shared in the Five Stages of Peak Performance. Just remember that it will take patience to make them a part of who you are.

There is more to Sheri's story than we initially shared. Six years after her embarrassing performance and decision to quit singing, she was now enrolled at the university and working on a piano degree when she decided to take Jon's class, the Psychology of Music

Performance. After sharing her story in class, Sheri began to apply
the tools from the Five Stages. With her new mindset, she saw her
embarrassing story in a different light and made a pivotal decision.

Two weeks later, as class started, she enthusiastically thrust her
hand into the air. With a radiant smile, she announced, "Dr. Skidmore, I just wanted you to know I sang a solo in church on Sunday
for the first time in years." The entire class cheered for her victory
and celebrated her newfound freedom to sing. It was exciting to see
how quickly she was able to break out of the old story and conquer
the deep anxiety stopping her from singing. Sheri experienced a
breakthrough because she was willing to take action and apply some
new tools to the beliefs she'd held on to from that old situation. She
was free to sing again!

We hope that, as it was for Sheri, this book will be a game-chang-
er for you and help you become more peaceful, confident, and bold.
We'd like to wrap things up with one of our favorite quotes by Ella
Wheeler Wilcox:

One ship sails East,
And another West,
By the self-same winds that blow,
'Tis the set of the sail
And not the gale,
That determines the way we go.

Like the winds of the sea
Are the waves of time,
As we journey along through life,
'Tis the set of the soul,
That determines the goal,
And not the calm or the strife.

We hope *Conquer Anxiety* will help you set your sail and catch
the wind that is at all of our backs. It really is the "set of the soul that
determines the goal, and not the calm or the strife."

Congratulations on investing the time and energy to finish this book. You've taken the first step on a lifelong journey of facing your anxiety and becoming your best.

We wish you the greatest success as you continue on the journey of life!

Endnotes

1. See Jacobson, E., 1938) Jacobson, E. (1938). Progressive relaxation. Chicago: University of Chicago Press
2. Tapping technique Craig, G (n.d.). EFT Manual (PDF). Archived from the original (PDF) on 2016-03-03.
3. (Daniel J.Seigel 2007) *The Mindful Brain: Reflection and Attunement in the Cultivation of Well-Being* (New York: WW Norton & Company, 2007)
4. (Silver, Gottman, 1994) Nan Silver; Gottman, John (1994). *Why Marriages Succeed or Fail: What You Can Learn from the Breakthrough Research to Make Your Marriage Last.* New York: Simon &
5. Shad Helmstetter, *What to Say When You Talk to Your Self* (Place: publisher, date), page number/s.
6. (J. Beck 2008) Beck, J. S. (2011). *Cognitive behavior therapy: Basics and beyond.* 2nd ed. New York: Guilford
7. Thomas Blackwell, *The Liberty of Our Language Revealed* (Place: publisher, 2018).
8. Broomhead, Paul, Jon B. Skidmore, Dennis L Eggett, Melissa M Mills. "The Effect of Positive Mindset Trigger Words on the Performance Expression of Non-Expert Adult Singers." Contributions to Music Education (2010): 65-86.

Citations

Yerks RM, Dodson JD (1908). "The relation of strength of stimulus to rapidity of habit – formation" Journal of Comparative nNeurology and Psychology. 18 (5): 459-482.

Mihaly Csikszentmihályi (1990). Flow: The Psychology of Optimal Experience. Harper & Row.

Sheldon Cohen, Denise Janicki-Deverts, William J. Doyle, Gregory E. Miller, Ellen Frank, Bruce S. Rabin, and Ronald B. Turner. Chronic stress, glucocorticoid receptor resistance, inflammation, and disease risk. PNAS, April 2, 2012 DOI: 10.1073/pnas.1118355109.

Additional Resources to Help You

1. Visit www.AnxietyConquer.com to:

- Access free videos.
- Invest in an online course that demonstrates how to do each of the exercises and activities listed in this book. This also includes downloadable worksheets you can use to practice many of the activities found in the Five Stages.

2. Join the *ConquerAnxiety* Facebook group. Use this group to get ideas from others and share your own insights. To join the group, simply go to Facebook and search for ConquerAnxiety.

3. Read *Becoming Your Best: The 12 Principles of Highly Successful Leaders* to get additional ideas that will help you live a more productive and fulfilled life.

About the Authors

JON SKIDMORE

As a performance coach, private practice psychologist and educator of nearly thirty years, Jon has helped thousands of people from around the world conquer their anxiety. As a young singer he was taught that a good performance was all about the practice. Then, as a singer and young psychologist, he learned that a peak performance is all about developing the mindset to equal the skill set. That realization changed Jon's life and that's when he decided to become a performance coach.

He had a vocal scholarship to Utah State University where he earned his bachelor's degree in psychology. He then earned a master's degree in counseling and guidance from Brigham Young University where he also sang with the BYU Singers. He then earned a doctoral degree in clinical psychology from the Chicago School of Professional Psychology. Jon did his doctoral dissertation on peak performance and how that applies to musicians. He is currently a practicing psychologist, specializing in anxiety disorders.

He presented his first peak performance workshop in 1986 and has worked with students from the local elementary school all the way to Juilliard. He's been teaching the class - The Psychology of Music Performance - at Brigham Young University since 1991.

ROB SHALLENBERGER

Rob is a highly sought after trainer and speaker. He is one of the world's leading authorities on high-performance and productivity. He's trained hundreds of organizations around the world and coached many successful leaders.

After spending two years of service in Bolivia, he attended Utah State University where he graduated in 2000 with a degree in Marketing. He went on to earn an MBA from Colorado State University.

He served as an F-16 Fighter Pilot in the Air Force for 11 years and during that time also worked as an Advance Agent for Air Force One travelling the world and coordinating with foreign embassies and the Secret Service.

He's the CEO of Becoming Your Best Global Leadership. His company released a national bestselling book titled *Becoming Your Best: The 12 Principles of Highly Successful Leaders* and *The Transformation Challenge: The Six-Steps to Planning and Execution.* He's also the author of the book *How to Succeed in High School* and a children's book titled *A-Z: The Best in You and Me.*

Rob considers his greatest accomplishment to be that he's been married for 22 years and has four beautiful children.

STEVEN SHALLENBERGER

Steve is well known as a global leader in high-performance research and training. He dedicated 40 years of research to identify the 12 principles of highly successful people and leaders. Based on that research, Steve founded Becoming Your Best Global leadership and developed numerous proprietary tools and processes to help develop high-performance people and teams. Becoming Your Best has launched multiple National Bestselling books and Steve has trained hundreds of groups around the world.

Through the years, Steve has accumulated four decades of business experience as a business owner, trusted senior executive, professional corporate trainer, and respected community leader. After graduating from Brigham Young University in 1976, Steve launched Eagle Systems International, a global leadership and management consulting firm. He has successfully led companies in four different industries.

During those formative years, he continued his education at the Harvard Business School. Steve also worked many years with Stephen R. Covey. As a key leader, among others, he helped build the world-renowned Covey Leadership Center.

Steve served as president of the Brigham Young University Alumni Association. He currently sits on the board of trustees for America's Freedom Foundation.

He has been married for 45 years and has six children.